A
SEASON
TO
HEAL

A SEASON TO HEAL

LUCI FREED &
PENNY YVONNE SALAZAR

CUMBERLAND HOUSE

PUBLISHING INC

Published by Cumberland House Publishing, Inc., 431 Harding Industrial Drive, Nashville, Tennessee, TN 37211.

All scripture quotations, unless otherwise indicated, are from the NEW KING JAMES VERSION of the Bible. Copyright © 1979, 1980, 1982, Thomas Nelson, Inc., Publishers.

Scripture quotations noted NIV are taken from the HOLY BIBLE, NEW INTERNATIONAL VERSION © Copyright © 1973, 1978, 1984 by International Bible Society. Used by permission of Zondervan Bible Publishing House. All rights reserved.

The "NIV" and "New International Version" trademarks are registered in the United States Patent and Trademark Office by International Bible Society. Use of either trademark requires the permission of International Bible Society.

In order to protect the privacy of the authors' clients, stories recorded in the book are composite illustrations from the case histories of several individuals.

Library of Congress Cataloging-in-Publication Data

Freed, Luci.
  A season to heal / Luci Freed & Penny Yvonne Salazar.
    p. cm.
  Originally published: Nashville : T. Nelson Publishers, c1993.
  Includes bibliographical references.
  ISBN 1-888952-10-5 (pbk. : alk. paper)
  1. Abortion--United States--Psychological aspects. 2. Abortion counseling--United States. I. Salazar, Penny Yvonne. II. Title.
HQ767.5.U5F74 1996
362.1'9888--dc20   96-30778
                                                        CIP

Printed in the United States of America
      5 6 7 8 9 — 03

We dedicate this book

to all the women

who have not yet grieved for their children

and to those children who have never been mourned.

CONTENTS

Acknowledgments

Preface

Introduction

Part 1: The Dilemma and the Damage

1. What Is Post-Abortion Stress? *1*
2. You Are Not Alone *13*
3. Broken Threads *27*

Part 2: The Road to Wholeness

4. The Healing Process *45*
5. Step Out of the Dark *53*
6. Recognize Real Feelings and Real Losses *65*
7. Cancel Empty Deals *71*
8. Unlock the Trapdoor of Guilt and Shame *79*
9. Take the Lid Off *91*
10. Do Not Surrender to Depression *103*
11. Find Freedom in Forgiveness *115*
12. Become Reconciled *129*

Part 3: Hope for the Journey

13. Where Do I Go from Here? *141*
Appendix A: The Twelve Steps of Alcoholics
    Anonymous *153*
Appendix B: Intensive Care *155*
Appendix C: Your Support Group *165*
Appendix D: References for Counseling *171*
Appendix E: References for Further Reading *173*

Notes *175*
About the Authors *177*

Acknowledgments

We would like to express our deepest gratitude to:

God for His faithfulness, lovingkindness, protection, and provision. We would not be where we are today if He had not turned our lives and hearts toward Him.

Ken for making the dream of this book a reality by believing in us and our message.

Bill, Jennifer, and Lonnie for their insight and expertise, without whom our thoughts would still be unfinished sentences and scrambled outlines.

Ron Pitkin and Cumberland House for making sure this book is available for all who need it.

All of the post-abortion women we have had the privilege to know for giving us your stories and allowing us to share in your lives. We will forever cherish you.

Our families, especially Luci's dad, John; Penny's husband, Kevin, and her son, Chris, for their love and sacrifice. We love you.

Cyndi, Lynn, Linda, Cathy, Nancy, Gidget, Sarah, Trisha, Cathy, Stacy, Christine, Margo, Lorie, and Don Finto for sharing in our personal journeys toward healing and for your steadfast friendship.

So many other unnamed but much-loved friends for your support and encouragement, especially on the days we thought we were empty. Looking back it's obvious that over and over again just the right person was there when we needed them.

Mr. and Mrs. Muellar, Mr. and Mrs. Creswell, Mr. and Mrs. Chapman, Mr. and Mrs. McWilliams, S. Mansfield, and C. Kiemle for providing us airfare and places to stay while we wrote.

Our capable, competent, and dedicated staff for doing their jobs as well as ours, while we were distracted by traveling and writing and rewriting and rewriting.

Our boards for giving us their blessing and the resources to complete this work.

Cleo Taplin, Kim Tant, Susan Bubbers, Kathy Wells, and Shawnie Dugan for your dancing fingers on the word processor. This truly wouldn't have been possible without you.

Carol Belles and L.K. Printing for their help with fax services and preparing the artwork for publishing.

Anne, Lortie, Davita Hungate, and Scott Kiemle for their artistic gifts. This book is greatly enhanced because of their ability to take the pictures from our heads and put them on the page.

To all of the songwriters and poets who shared their words and their messages. You have helped all the words in this book come alive.

We call our lives blessed because of you, and we know we would not be complete without each and every one of you.

Preface

Abortion affects a woman's life long after the actual event has taken place. The woman who has had an abortion experiences a significant loss. Every woman deals with that loss differently, often even denying it exists. She struggles with a pain deep inside her heart. Hers is a silent pain, felt in secret—the grief for a lost child.

Through our counseling, we have seen hundreds of women struggling with emotional pain after their abortions. Their specific stories are different, yet they all hold common sorrows. And over the years, as these women have shared their stories with us and with one another, the burdens, the anger, and the emotional pain have eased. They have begun to heal, and offer their stories as part of this book.

Our hearts ache for the countless women who still suffer and are yet to begin the restoration process in their own lives. We hope this book will offer you a road map through the valley of grief. Moving through your grief will be difficult at certain points, but as a result you will find comfort, hope, strength, and purpose in your life.

Our prayers are with you as you begin your journey.

Introduction

This book is about coming to peace with a painful reality in your life. It's about grieving and inner healing.

Grieving your abortion losses is one of the most important tasks you will do in your lifetime. It starts as you stop denying your pain, and it continues until you reach a point of reconciliation.

None of this happens overnight. It takes a season to heal, not a moment or a lifetime. As there is purpose to each season there is purpose in this healing process. Every season does come to an end.

Inner healing is not just reducing your pain. Ultimately, it is self-acceptance and forgiveness, a reclaiming of the inner beauty God has given you. Coming to a place of peace and experiencing inner healing is unconditional self-love.

We believe two things will help you during this grieving process. First, finding support is crucial. Since people approach healing differently, what works for someone else may not work for you. You may need support from another individual or from a larger group. The affirmation of God's love may be your source of strength, or you may need the prayers of others to help "bathe" you as you work through the book and grieve. Appendix B is designed to help you in finding someone to assist you in your journey.

Second, we suggest that you keep a journal as you do your grief work. Throughout the book we encourage you to do some introspective exploring, because putting your thoughts and feelings down on paper is therapeutic—and confidential. Part of healing is in the acknowledgment of your inner feelings and thoughts.

As you look at how your abortion has affected your life and as you name and grieve your losses, know that we honor your courage.

PART ONE

❧

The Dilemma

---

and

---

the Damage

CHAPTER ONE

What Is Post-Abortion Stress?

The college cafeteria buzzed with students grabbing a quick lunch between classes. Patty and Bob sat at a table alone. She picked at her food as Bob spoke emphatically.

"You know, Patty, it was really the best thing for both of us at this point in our lives. We couldn't handle a baby right now. We need to finish college, and I've got a great grad school offer. You know I can't get a good job without another degree," he said, leaning closer. "Sure, we can get married in a few years, but we need to get our feet on the ground before we start a family."

Bob paused to see how Patty would react. They had gone to the abortion clinic three weeks ago, and Patty had felt confused about their decision ever since. Was it the best thing to do? Was the problem really solved? The questions annoyed Bob. After all, whether the abortion was right or wrong, it was done.

Patty opened her mouth to speak, but Bob interrupted, not wanting to hear the same things again.

"You said your folks would have been devastated. Well, how could we do that to them? We really did the right thing, hon." He shrugged his shoulders and shoveled the last bite of pie into his mouth. He continued between chews, "I'm tired of talking about this all the time, and I'm tired of you being depressed. You gotta get over this."

"Hi, guys. What's up?" a friend called from two tables over. Bob got up and motioned for Patty to come with him to join their friends, but Patty didn't move.

Bob obviously didn't understand. She dropped the subject . . . for now.

Movies, classes, part-time jobs, and college life in general occupied most of Patty's time for a long while after that day. Although tiny doubts still scratched away in the back of her mind, she kept her confusion and questions to herself.

Finally, after several months, she thought she would burst. One night she confided in her roommate, Marcy, as they sat in the dorm, studying for the next day's calculus exam. The room had been unusually quiet for several minutes when Patty broke the silence.

"You know, I had an abortion last semester," she said, a little too casually.

"Oh, really? I've had one too."

Patty looked up, surprised. Marcy too? That gave her the courage to say what was really on her mind: "I've sort of felt weird about it, actually. My parents taught me that abortion was wrong, and they would just freak out if they knew."

Marcy answered, "Oh, it's no big deal. They don't *have* to know. We can always have babies later when we're through with school. Then we'll be better able to provide for a baby. It just wouldn't work now." She laughed, dismissing Patty's questions with a wave of her hand. How silly to be worried about the abortion now, Marcy seemed to imply.

Patty went back to her calculus, but her doubts would not be stilled. Now, she was even more confused.

They must be right, Patty reasoned finally. She shouldn't be wondering and worrying about the abortion so much. Maybe she had been taught that abortion was wrong and that life began at conception, but she certainly hadn't felt any signs of life inside her before the procedure.

And Bob was right: Her folks would have been devastated. They had no idea she was even sexually active. Now they wouldn't have to know about any of it. It was the best thing for everyone concerned.

I need to snap out of it and get on with my life, Patty decided. *I'm spending way too much time dwelling on this. It's not a big deal to Marcy. She seems to handle her abortion fine, and I should too. Actually I know a lot of girls who have had abortions, and they're all perfectly fine. I must be the weird one.*

But no matter how hard she tried, Patty could not push her thoughts and feelings aside. She felt alone, with no one to share her doubts. *She didn't know that the pain she felt had a name and that she was* not *alone.* Many other women have had thoughts and feelings like Patty's and also heard that they should "get over it."

FINALLY A NAME: PTSD

Naming something—whether a problem or a disease—always seems to help. If you've ever had mysterious symptoms, you probably could handle it a little better when you finally heard, "This is what the problem is. It has a name and real symptoms."

What Patty and millions of other women experience is known as Post-Abortion Stress (PAS). PAS is a particular form of a larger diagnosis known as Post Traumatic Stress Disorder (PTSD). Veterans often experience this disorder after enduring horrible traumas during war. The suffering of Vietnam veterans first brought PTSD to public attention. These soldiers returned to a country that had ambivalent feelings about the war they fought. Americans did not want to acknowledge the experiences of the veterans because they thought the war was unnecessary. No one in America, the country these soldiers fought to protect and save, wanted to hear anything about what had happened to them "over there."

Vietnam veterans felt alone with no one to talk to. They couldn't mention the war that had caused them so much pain, and they couldn't discuss the atrocities, the torture, or the loneliness. So many Vietnam veterans kept secrets, turned inward, and became angry and bitter. Some of them also hid behind an emotional wall to protect themselves and to survive in a world that did not understand their pain.

Finally, a few therapists realized that these returning soldiers needed help. Veterans and other concerned citizens struggled to help our society become aware of returning soldiers' needs. Besides counseling and public awareness, the effort was finally made to build a Vietnam War Memorial, a place where America could give credibility to the efforts and deaths of war victims. The memorial we have come to know as "The Wall" provides a place for American veterans and family members to remember and to grieve.

Press coverage of tragedies related to PTSD has educated therapists and the public and made us more willing to recognize and deal with PTSD. We realize now that survivors of airline crashes and earthquakes also frequently experience PTSD.

POST-ABORTION STRESS

Specifically, Post-Abortion Stress is a stress reaction experienced by some women after their abortions. The onset of this reaction can occur anytime from immediately after the procedure to several years later. Much like PTSD, Post-Abortion Stress is caused by a woman's inability to express her feelings surrounding her pregnancy and abortion. In addition, the woman is not able to resolve her losses and to come to a place of inner peace.

The PAS victim's inability to handle her feelings is reinforced by many factors: the crisis surrounding her pregnancy; the urgency she felt in making a decision; the absence of a viable support system; the secrets she has kept; and the denial about recognizing and resolving her losses.

As with the Vietnam War, our country seems polarized about abortion. From both sides and for different reasons, women get loud messages that say, "Don't talk about it. Don't think about it. Get over it. Go on with life." A woman may be told by a pro-lifer that she has committed murder, the ultimate sin; she then believes that she can never find forgiveness. So she keeps her secret from friends at school, work, and church—always afraid that someone will find out. And she struggles with the consequences of her abortion *alone.*

Pro-choice advocates promote the importance of a woman's choice: her body, her future. Furthermore, they contend that the decision was the best one possible at the time and that afterwards a woman should put the abortion behind her and get on with life. Often the existence of PAS and any feelings of loss connected with her abortion are denied, because to acknowledge the loss is an issue they do not want to face.

Thus, people on both sides of the abortion issue silently give a post-abortion woman the same message: deny that her abortion had any effect on her life. Denial helps us cope with loss or trauma, because the human psyche can take only so much stress before it shuts down. Denial says, "This is not happening" or "This did not happen." Denial helps us handle a piece of the pain at a time. A husband whose wife is killed in a car wreck may not believe she is really gone. A woman who didn't want to be pregnant may not acknowledge her loss. Denial gives us a way to survive our immediate pain, but sooner or later, we must realize—and accept—that we have suffered loss. It is vital that losses be grieved in a healthy way.

PAS develops because a woman has not expressed her feelings and resolved her losses. She shuts her emotions down and develops coping mechanisms in order to survive. Until there is a crack in the wall of denial, or until she finds safe help, she is stuck. Much like a cancer left untreated, PAS continues to grow. A cancerous tumor must be removed and treated so that the body will heal. Likewise, PAS must be dealt with so that healing can take place.

SYMPTOMS OF POST-ABORTION STRESS

Symptoms accompany any disorder whether emotional or physical. By recognizing symptoms, professionals can name a disease or syndrome and begin to treat it. Recognizing symptoms of PAS will enable you and others who share your experience to break the isolation that fuels PAS. Until Patty found someone who shared her feelings, her isolation increased her anxiety.

Following is a list of common PAS symptoms. This composite list of symptoms is from a survey given to post-abortion women. Not all women experience all the symptoms; some women experience only a few; others identify with many of them. The onset of these symptoms may be immediate or delayed for many years after the abortion. This alphabetical list starts with common Post Traumatic Stress Disorder symptoms and then lists those more specific to Post-Abortion Stress. Do you identify with any of these symptoms?

General PTSD and PAS Symptoms

- Alcohol and/or drug abuse (usually to dull painful emotions or escape reality)
- Anger (often generalized or specifically aimed at those who were involved in the experience)
- Anxiety (probably non-specific or in form of a panic attack)
- Brief psychosis (a loss of reality lasting for a few days)
- Denial/repression (the "pushing down" of intolerable emotions)
- Depression
- Deterioration of self-concept (self-worth, self-image)
- Disruption in relationships (increasing inability to be intimate or social with friends and family)
- Disturbance in sleep patterns (sleeping more or less than usual)
- Feelings of helplessness or powerlessness
- Grief (Specific or non-specific)

- Guilt
- Isolation (staying alone more than usual)
- Nightmares or flashbacks
- Panic (or sense of being out of control)
- Psychological numbing (a diminished ability to experience any emotion)
- Regret
- Remorse
- Suicide thoughts or attempts

Specific PAS Symptoms

- Anniversary syndrome (an increase of symptoms around anniversary dates: the abortion and/or due date of the aborted baby)
- Anxiety over infertility
- Avoidance behaviors (avoiding any person or situation—pregnant friends, infants, vaginal exams, etc.—which could trigger abortion-related emotions)
- Eating disorders (becoming overweight or underweight to "protect" oneself against a possible future pregnancy; expression of self-hatred)
- Inability to bond with your children
- Preoccupation with becoming pregnant again (an attempt to replace the aborted baby)
- Psychosexual disorders (inability to engage in sexual activity or sexually acting out)
- Sudden, uncontrollable crying

Sometimes people or situations trigger PAS symptoms. It is as if something or someone has pushed a button that releases thoughts and feelings you thought long-buried. Some of the more common triggers are: the people or things that remind you of your abortion; news coverage about the issue; the anniversary date of the time you conceived, the date of your abortion or the date your baby would have been born; people or things that remind you of being pregnant, babies or small children; other losses in your life or holidays. Suddenly, the issue of the abortion comes to the front of your mind again.

WOMEN AT RISK

Potentially any woman who has had an abortion is at risk for PAS. All that is necessary for development of PAS is for a woman not to face her emotions and not grieve her loss. Circumstances and personality also play a large part in how women deal with loss issues in life.

We believe women vary in the intensity of their emotions and the severity of their symptoms. However, our experience has been that certain women may be at higher risk for developing PAS: teenagers, women who already have children, women who have second trimester abortions, women who feel pressured by circumstances, and women struggling with value conflicts.

The first group of women at risk for PAS is teenagers. Often the world of a teenager can prevent a young woman from exploring deeply the meaning of an abortion and the impact it will have on her future. She had not yet realized how early decisions could affect her so deeply later.

Janice had an abortion when she was seventeen. Her high school activities, active social life, and after-school job kept her busy and happy, so she never gave her abortion a second thought. Janice certainly would never have described feelings of sadness or loss at that time in her life.

When Janice turned twenty-three, however, she began to notice media reports that focused heavily on abortion. Her own abortion came to mind, and she then questioned things she used to believe. Maybe there had been other options. Was it a baby or a fetus? What would life have been like if she had decided to have the baby? Were her new feelings of regret a signal of her need to grieve for her lost baby?

A second group of women at risk are those who already have children when they choose to have abortions. Their reasons are as different as the women themselves. Like most mothers, these women love, care for, protect, and make sacrifices for their children. This natural instinct to protect their young, in fact, becomes a thorn to mothers who abort. The need to grieve their loss lies very close to the surface.

Society allows many rituals to help us grieve the death of our loved ones. In recent years, we have taken important strides in seeing that women grieve stillborn children and babies lost through miscarriage. But there is still little visible support for helping the mother who has had an abortion.

The third group at higher risk of developing PAS are those women who delay their abortion procedure until the second and third trimesters. This would also include abortions done for medical reasons or fetal abnormalities. The factors that make abortion so difficult for these women are the advanced stage of fetal development, the increased risk of medical complications for the mother, and the greater likelihood of the mother coming into contact with her aborted child, if the child somehow "survives" the abortion procedure and lives for even a short while.

Sherry had borne three healthy children already when an ultrasound in her fourth pregnancy showed "signs of problems." So in her sixteenth week the doctor suggested an amniocentesis. Because of the potential danger in this procedure, Sherry sought a second opinion. By the time she then had the amniocentesis, she was five months pregnant.

Two doctors recommended abortion, saying that the test showed gross abnormalities and that the baby would die soon after birth. Sherry and her husband talked with their pastor and trusted friends and decided on abortion. Upon examination of the baby after the procedure, the doctors indeed found some fetal abnormalities. Still, Sherry and her husband struggled with their grief, their choice, and the advice given them.

Many of the stories we hear every day in our offices are from women who were themselves ambivalent but felt pressured into their abortion decision. This is the fourth group of women at risk. We hear these remarks often: "My parents insisted I get an abortion." "My boyfriend said the relationship was over if I didn't abort the baby." "I never wanted the abortion, but I just couldn't afford another child." "When I found out I was pregnant I was really happy—excited, you know? Then everything fell apart. I had no choice."

These women felt pressured and trapped. Their situations put them in a position that conflicted with their own desires. Getting an abortion under pressure brings up struggles in addition to loss, that center around choice and control over your life and the ability to make positive decisions on your own.

A fifth group of women who struggle with PAS are those who experience a conflict of values. We learn our value system from different sources: our families, our culture, our faith. Where we form our values makes little difference when our choices fall outside these boundaries. Deciding to get an abortion often comes into sharp opposition with the strong life ethic of some women. The struggle to resolve feelings and loss becomes more intense when women are already in conflict about their value systems. For example, Patty's early training about the value of life created inner conflict when she had an abortion. One of the questions she kept asking herself was whether her decision was right or wrong.

Patty, Janice, Sherry, and possibly you experience feelings of conflict that continue until someone is found to listen and validate your feelings. You need to hear these words: "Yes, that's right. Your feelings and fears are legitimate. You did experience a loss. Yes, you do need to grieve." What freedom they feel at that point—the freedom to express themselves in a *safe* place.

As Patty herself explained: "Although I wasn't sure how to talk about my feelings, I felt safe enough the first day to tell part of my story. My counselor validated my feelings and my worth as a person. The next week I risked telling a little more. She asked me to remember and to tell her about things I had desperately pushed away. So I did. And I finally allowed myself to feel sorrow, pain, and loss. The counselor did not condemn me or tell me I was a terrible person for doing what

I had done. She let me talk as much as I wanted to about the abortion, and she wasn't afraid of my emotions. It helped so much to finally have someone understand."

Post-Abortion Stress is real, and women who have experienced these fears and anxieties need to know that they are not alone. Despite the misinformation and misconceptions, abortion affects women's lives. Acknowledgment of this fact alone can be the beginning of a woman's journey toward healing.

This acknowledgment and beginning are enough right now to help you continue and enough to give you hope.

CHAPTER TWO

You Are Not Alone

Nancy came into Luci's office, sat down on the striped sofa near the door, and looked her straight in the eyes as she talked: "I only came to see you because my friend Fran says you've helped her a lot. She picked me up from work today so we could come together."

The slender eighteen-year-old propped one elbow on the padded arm of the sofa. Nancy was dressed in stylish jeans with a rugby shirt. At first glance she appeared very confident; however, she seemed unsure of what to say next and slowly twisted a curl of brown hair around her right index finger.

Then she blurted out, "I'm really getting scared of myself and my drinking. I want to be drunk all the time, and it takes more and more alcohol to make me feel better.

"Last week I tried pure grain alcohol because some girl I was talking to at a party said it was great. Well, it wasn't great for me. I had a terrible reaction and started yelling and screaming at every guy there. And then I got sick. Fran saw the whole thing. She says I'm really scaring her lately, too.

"That night was awful. The next day I couldn't function. Thank goodness I spent the night with Fran so I didn't have to deal with my mom; that would have been *too* much—the last straw."

Nancy looked down and began to pick at her fingernail. She seemed a little nervous.

"So you and your mom don't get along," Luci commented.

Nancy answered angrily, "I'm the child they're disappointed in. My brother and sister do all the right stuff to make my folks happy. I can't do anything right. I want to run away, and I'm sure they wish I would. I'm tired of trying to please them because nothing works."

Luci tried another approach. "When did you start drinking?"

"Oh, I always had a little at parties, y'know. Everybody does. But only on weekends. After Joey and I started dating, we rarely drank."

"Oh? Tell me about Joey."

Her eyes dropped and she took a while to answer. Her hands went still in her lap. "We broke up on February 1."

And then her story began to unravel . . . Nancy had always felt like the lost, insignificant child. Her older brother was a star athlete, very popular, and her dad's favorite child. Nancy's sister was a straight A student and did some modeling; their mother was always comparing Nancy and her sister. Nancy disagreed often with her parents about rules. She liked to have a good time and wasn't very studious. Truthfully, she hated school; it was too structured and Nancy claimed she was bored by it. But Joey, whom she met in July, seemed to fill a void in her life. She loved being with him, and when he pushed her to sleep with him, it seemed natural to her. He made her feel so alive; she really thought he was special.

Then Nancy missed her period in November, and two weeks before Christmas, she and Joey went to a clinic to get a pregnancy test. It was positive, and they were scared. Joey was a high school junior with strict parents. How could he tell them? And Nancy knew it would be the final blow for her folks—and right at Christmas. So they told no one.

Joey and Nancy both had after-school jobs, so they pooled their money, made an appointment, and silently drove to the abortion clinic on a Friday. She knew her folks were going to a big holiday party that night and would be out late. And she wasn't scheduled to work at a mall restaurant until the late shift Saturday evening. The clinic said she'd be fine by then. Perfect timing—she could rest until then in her room, and no one would find out.

Everything proceeded according to her plan. She got through that Friday and the rest of the holidays. She and Joey didn't talk about the abortion again, but somehow things were different between them. They began fighting, and by the week after New Year's, he quit calling. So Nancy called him begging to see him again. But all he would say was that he didn't want to be with her right now—maybe when things "settled down." And Nancy wasn't sure what *that* was supposed to mean.

ISOLATION

After a few weeks, Nancy gave up on Joey and accepted an invitation to a party with friends. The host's parents were out of town for a few days, and the kids got hold of several cases of beer. It was downhill from there. Nancy drank most of that weekend and every weekend after. Some girls taught her how to sneak beer into her locker at school like they did. Very soon, alcohol became a part of her daily life.

And so did anger and lying. She now had more and more things to hide from her parents. Her grades dropped, and she barely graduated. That summer was one big party. When she wasn't out, Nancy locked herself in her bedroom. Predictably, the fights with her mom also increased. Nancy felt so isolated as well as an utter disappointment to her folks. She didn't feel there had been any choice except having the abortion and keeping it a secret forever. *So* staying drunk covered up her increasing sense of inadequacy, hopelessness, and failure.

When Fran confronted Nancy about the increase in her drinking, plus her constant angry rage, Nancy finally began to look at herself. She realized that there were definite changes in her behavior, that she was drinking too much, and that most of the time she was angry at everything and everybody.

Nancy already felt so bad about herself and her relationships that she didn't realize how the decision to abort had added to her stress until she began counseling. Drinking, low self-esteem, anger, and rage were all symptoms of a deeper pain and need. However, nothing she tried helped ease her pain until Fran, out of love and support, confronted her and brought her to Luci's office.

Nancy had learned very few healthy coping skills. She did not express her emotions, so her mom and dad did not understand Nancy or her pain. Although adolescence is a time of preparation for adulthood, Nancy was stuck emotionally. Her life was filled with fear, insecurity, lack of guidance, and misunderstanding. Fortunately, she realized that her behavior was out of control, so eight months after her abortion, Nancy came in for counseling.

MONIQUE

Not everyone finds help so soon. It took Monique many years to make the first step. Monique told us her story:

"The smiling nurse looked at me and said, 'Congratulations, Monique. You're pregnant.'"

"Congratulations?" You must be kidding! What am I going to do? What will Peter say? I know he won't marry me. How will I be able to provide for three kids by myself? It's hard enough now with two. What will my family say? All of these thoughts flooded my mind as I smiled back and tried to swallow my tears. I had to get away from the doctor's office and think. I was scared; I couldn't believe I was really pregnant.

"Well, I told two people: Peter and my boss. Peter said, 'You should probably get an abortion. I'll give you the money.' And my boss told me I would probably lose my job if I didn't get an abortion.

"There was no way to tell my family. I had already been married once, to the father of my two children. He drank a lot and was physically abusive to me. My family helped me get out of that situation. Peter was abusive too, and my family was really disappointed about this relationship. I didn't see how I could tell them I was pregnant again. They had helped me so much already."

TRAPPED

She continued, "I remember the night before I got the abortion. I was taking a shower, feeling angry and trapped. Suddenly I started crying, and the tears wouldn't stop. I got so mad that I put my fist through the bathroom window. Peter lay in bed and didn't do *anything*. I know he had to have heard me. When I came to bed, he turned away from me. I needed someone to hold me, but no one did.

"Peter left on a business trip the next day, so I went to the clinic alone. The night after my abortion, I began to hemorrhage; I finally had to take a taxi to the county hospital. I can't remember ever feeling so alone and helpless. I missed two weeks of work. Peter called a couple of times, but I didn't want to talk to him. I finally told him to come and get all his stuff out of my place and leave the key. After that it was months before I heard from him again.

"I raised my kids, had a career, and went to church every week. Then I married again to a very compassionate, loving man, but I had a few affairs anyway. I just felt empty and anxious all the time. In all those years, I never told anyone about the abortion. Oh, I talked about it to God. Every day I asked Him to forgive me—every day for twenty-six years.

"Finally, at age fifty-one, I decided to try a counselor. I saw him for a couple of years. I did mention the abortion in recounting my history, but he never asked me about it again. When I brought it up myself, he said it had nothing to do with my current problems. Somehow, I didn't believe him.

"I also talked with my pastor several times. He was a good man and told me God had forgiven me. I couldn't believe that was true about *me*. My sin was too big for God to forgive. The pastor then gave me the name of a woman who did post-abortion counseling and suggested I see her."

Monique called Penny's office and asked a lot of questions about the counseling we provide for women who have had abortions. For the first few visits Monique wore black clothes and dark glasses, kept her coat on, and sat right next to the door. She had trouble trusting that anything or anyone would help her. Monique wasn't sure she would even know how to live without her depression. Monique's life had focused on raising her two children and making a career. She also had had several different relationships, tried counseling, yet she always had a nagging, anxious feeling.

Like Monique, most women carry the emotional pain from their abortion for a long time, and they frequently carry it alone. If they have told anyone, it was in strictest confidence. Renee's story was different, but she also carried her secret for a long time.

RENEE

It was Monday night at the counseling center, seven women and two facilitators were ready for the first session of a post-abortion support group. They all sat in a circle around the sitting room behind the counseling office.

As they introduced themselves, most of the women began to relax, but Penny could sense Renee's apprehension growing. Renee's doctor had referred her to the group, thinking that a group might help answer the questions and doubts she was struggling with.

Renee had been twenty and home from her first year of college when she discovered she was pregnant. She was still dating her high school boyfriend, although her parents had always thought he was far beneath her. She had a tremendous musical talent, excellent grades in school, and a great future ahead of her—if she would just "dump that boy" (their words).

Renee's dad had built a business and was one of the city's most powerful and influential men. He provided his beautiful wife and two daughters with everything their hearts desired: a tennis court, swimming pool, ski boat, private schools, lovely clothes, and cars for the girls when they turned sixteen.

Mom went to a weekly Bible study and regularly attended church. She raised her two daughters to be conservative, responsible people: Abortion rarely crossed her mind. Why should it? She had a close relationship with her girls, and she never thought they'd get pregnant before they got married.

HOW COULD YOU?

The night Renee told her parents she was pregnant, her dad hit the roof. He insisted she get an abortion . . . *now*. An unwed mother in his family could ruin his business reputation and social standing. And he refused to have a grandchild fathered by *that* boy. They argued far into the night. Renee cried, her dad yelled, and Mom wrung her hands. Dad won, and two days later it was over.

Everyone, including Renee, was relieved that it was done. The whole family took a trip to the beach for a week, and everyone went back to life as it had been. Of course, Dad refused to let Renee see her boyfriend. Renee tried to obey her dad since she felt so ashamed that she had caused him so much trouble. Then one weekend, when a friend's parents were out of town, Renee stayed there a few days and used the time to see and talk things over with her boyfriend. Renee and her boyfriend talked all night, and they both realized they had to break it off.

Renee returned to college that fall, keeping her secret from her friends. She was a beautiful girl and had lots of dates and friends. She threw herself into her studies and her music. After graduation, when an offer came to play oboe with a well-known orchestra, she left in July for the West Coast.

Renee fit into the orchestra easily. She made new friends quickly and continued to date. Her career was off to a great start when she found herself pregnant—again. This time, she knew she would abort. She'd done it before; why shouldn't she do it again? And besides, her family would be so disappointed over another pregnancy outside of marriage. They had her "perfect future" all planned. She would meet a handsome, stable man who could provide the lifestyle she had always known; she could continue her career if she wished, have a lovely home with lovely children, . . . and live "happily ever after."

Renee didn't tell anyone about this abortion—not family, not friends, not colleagues, not even the father of the baby. She made an appointment with a private physician and then returned to life as usual.

The storybook man, Frederic, did come along. Their wedding was a big event, and all their friends and family wished them well. Renee and Frederic bought a beautiful, four-bedroom home in an exclusive neighborhood. They joined the country club and circulated in the "best" social circles. Their life could hardly have been more perfect. A couple of years later, they decided to start a family. It didn't take long before their efforts were rewarded.

In her fourteenth week, Renee's first ultrasound let her see the baby on video. Renee and Frederic watched the pictures over and over, and their friends and family shared their excitement.

But a vague sense of doubt began to creep into Renee's mind. She found herself sitting with her hands on her growing tummy, thinking about her aborted babies. Had they really been her children? She had never thought about it before. Why now?

Did those babies look like this one did at fourteen weeks? Did a wanted, loved baby and an unwanted, unloved baby look the same on ultrasound? She believed this baby was alive and growing, and she was excited about daily changes in her body and the baby. What was the difference? The questions bothered her, but she kept them to herself.

When their beautiful baby girl was born, Renee and Frederic were delighted, but deep inside Renee wondered more than ever about the two abortions. She often moped around the house in a melancholy mood, trying to sort out her feelings. Would the children have looked like this one? How old would they be? Would they like the same things as this adorable, soft child in her arms?

For many women, becoming pregnant is not a joyous occasion. Like Monique, Nancy, and Renee, the reality of being pregnant collides head-on with the cold, hard facts of life—cold hard facts that have never been quite as strong or heavy before. Circumstances do not always make a pregnancy easy. As women sift through their options and feelings, more than one million a year decide to get abortions.

What happens next? Relief. Sadness. Numbness. A return to the old life. Maybe striving for a new life.

Where do these women put their experience? Some put their abortion behind them, as something they wish to forget. Others hold it in front of them, as a reminder to be more careful. Still others carry the experience on their shoulders, as a burden to live with. Some may shove the memory into a hiding place, never to be looked at or felt again.

This is why we have told you the stories of Monique, Nancy, and Renee. We want you to know that there are no stereotypes of women who get abortions, no typical reasons for their abortions, and no standard feelings that they experience after their abortion. In America, one out of four women has had an abortion. They are teenagers, twenty, thirty, or older. They are single, married, in good and bad relationships. They are black, white, Hispanic, Asian, Native American. They are wealthy, poor, or in the middle class. They may have children or be childless.

Before and after their abortions, these women live on every street, go to public or private high school, attend college, have successful careers, shop at the grocery store, attend church, have dreams and great potential. They may fill their lives with family gatherings on Sundays and holidays, nice vacations, movies, parties, and friends. There is no way to outwardly detect which woman in the mall carries the pain of an abortion under the surface.

However, our experience and research suggest common threads that run through the abortion experience of most women. We will cover two related themes in this chapter: "secret-keeping" and "living behind a wall."

SECRET-KEEPING

Secret-keeping can distort lives in powerful ways, because the truth itself becomes unclear. Statements such as these become common: "If no one else knows what happened, then it didn't really happen"; "I can pretend that everything is okay." But the longer we keep the secret, the more severe the distortion grows. Think of it as moving through a house of mirrors, where you see your body in all sorts of shapes and sizes. After seeing all those images, you are not quite sure what your body really looks like. Secret-keeping brings a similar distortion to reality. After a while you are not really sure how you feel or how you should feel.

Another factor that pushes us to keep abortion secret is society's extreme polarization around abortion. Most people feel strongly one way or another about this issue. Politicians and the media play up the extreme emotions people have: hardly a day goes by when we don't hear about abortion in the news. Someone's for it; someone's against it. Someone acted violently against someone in the other camp. Whole families may be split over this issue.

Many life experiences that we once felt ashamed of have "come out of the closet." Divorce, alcoholism, and incest affect many of us and have become public issues. As our society has examined these issues and their emotional baggage, victims have begun to tell their stories and express their feelings. Opening themselves up to grief and healing has led these individuals into making healthier choices and changing their lives for the better.

Where does that leave the woman who chooses abortion? How will she work out her inner feelings? In a land where the law says abortion is okay or in a clinic where no one mentions what post-abortion reactions she might have, she is left alone to assume her feelings are abnormal. She feels crazy for having doubts or regrets. No one seems to understand her combination of relief and anxiety. How can she feel both ways at once? She has no place to turn, to speak about her loss either at the time of its occurence or years later when she notices that something is wrong. The struggle itself becomes her secret, one which she bears alone, maybe for many years, like Monique and Renee.

The secret was so important to Monique that she came to Penny's office under an assumed name and wearing a disguise. Renee kept her second abortion a secret from her family and also the father of her baby. She never told her husband about either abortion until she started to attend a recovery group. Nancy's secret propelled her into some very dangerous behavior. However, even as her drinking and the fighting with her mom escalated, so did her isolation. Her life was out of control, yet she shut out anyone who could help her.

LIVING BEHIND THE WALL

Many women live their lives after their abortions isolated behind a wall, locked up with their secrets, feelings, and thoughts. These women developed defense mechanisms to protect themselves from the pain that resulted from their abortions. They needed to function in the world outside, so they built a wall and hid what really matters inside.

No one was there to hear each woman's frustrations when she had her abortion; no one validated her feelings. With each brick she places on the wall, she convinces herself the abortion didn't happen or that it wasn't a big deal.

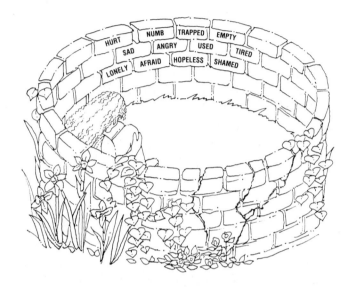

Often, this isolation is not apparent to the person living behind the wall or to the significant others in her life. This way of living becomes her "normal" lifestyle. In fact, if a woman has lived long enough behind her wall, she may not even remember her life outside that wall. She feels that people have let her down when she needed them and probably not just when she aborted, so she builds up the protective wall even higher and stronger. It takes a lot of emotional energy to hold up that wall; a person has to work very hard to keep it "looking good."

One day, however, the wall begins to crack. Sometimes the cracks are so small a woman doesn't notice them for a while. Renee didn't notice until she finally delivered a baby she wanted. Monique hid her cracks deep within her heart and questioned if the abortion was even the source of her pain. Nancy's wall crumbled under the violent force of her anger and drinking. As the cracks in the wall take shape, though, women begin to ask questions they never allowed themselves to ask. Doubts about their choices begin to nag, and buried feelings bubble to the surface.

STARTING THE GRIEVING PROCESS

Secret-keeping and living behind a wall are signs that a woman has not grieved in a healthy way. At first, she may keep her fears to herself. With the passage of time, she may finally talk with someone she trusts. Eventually, she will be ready to start the grieving process with a counselor, in a recovery group, or maybe just by reading this book.

After all those years of secret-keeping, Monique could see that the abortion did have significant implications and could have caused her pain and depression. Monique was ready to work, but it was several weeks before the dark glasses and dark clothes disappeared—longer than that before she trusted enough to share her real name. When she came for her last appointment—in bright clothes, pretty makeup, and a confident attitude—she looked like a different woman.

As the women in the support group shared their stories during the nine weeks they met, Renee began to acknowledge some of the emotions about her family that she had tried to forget. She had kept herself busy with things and people, and that had helped until now. Now she wanted to know, feel, and grieve for her two lost children. She also needed to talk to her husband and to be honest and open about her past. Later, Renee could visit her parents to talk about her feelings and to ask about theirs. They had forced her to keep the secret, because their dreams for their little girl were very important to them. Now her mom's heart was soft, and she was more than ready to grieve with Renee. Her dad—well, he wasn't quite as ready, but Renee hopes in time he will be.

As for Nancy, working through the abortion issue was wonderfully healing. She felt relief and the freedom *not* to drink anymore. Counseling also brought up those other problems that were there long before the abortion. Because of her dysfunctional family, Nancy is in group therapy learning how to stop those recurring problems in her life and in the lives of her future children. She is learning to choose healthy relationships and trust again.

Like Monique, Renee, and Nancy, many other women have grieved their abortion losses in a healthy way. They too have been able to unburden themselves and live life differently. If you choose to work through the material in this book and grieve your losses, we know that you can experience a new beginning in your life. In the next chapter we will begin to look specifically at how your abortion has affected your life.

CHAPTER THREE

Broken Threads

For twenty-six years after her abortion, Monique hated herself. As Monique watched her two children grow into talented adults, she was plagued by thoughts of what her aborted child might have been like. The loss of this child weighed heavily on her mind. Monique's inability to forgive herself fueled her depression and isolation long after her abortion. She felt that getting pregnant was all her fault, and she continually berated herself for not standing up under the pressure of her circumstances. Monique reminded herself of all the things she should have done to prevent the pregnancy, the abortion, and her problems with men. She talked herself into believing that everyone else saw her as she saw herself: a failure.

When Patty decided to get an abortion in college, she struggled with the value system of her parents. Her boyfriend, Bob, had never thought about the issue, so he had trouble understanding Patty's continuing struggle. Over time her conflict of values intensified.

Nancy hit an emotional overload immediately after her abortion. Anger controlled her, and although that gave Nancy a feeling of power, the rage kept people from getting close to her. Her anger motivated most of her daily actions; she picked fights with everyone. It didn't take very long before Nancy began taking her anger out on herself. Within a few short months she went from drinking a little too much to becoming controlled by alcohol.

LEVELS OF IMPACT

Abortions affected each of these women on a different level. Monique struggled psychologically and emotionally. Patty's conflict was spiritual in nature, while Nancy was hit emotionally, relationally, and physically.

We believe that abortion affects every woman who has one. These effects manifest themselves in different ways, since each of us is made up of several separate but interconnected threads: psychological, emotional, physical, spiritual, relational, and sexual. Although we will discuss each of these threads separately, they are intricately and beautifully woven together with your life experiences to complete the complex masterpiece called a human being. We hope this illustration will help you to see how your abortion has shaped your life and influenced your decisions. We also want to explore how your primary needs for healthy relationships and a sense of significance are being blocked and how that relates to your abortion.

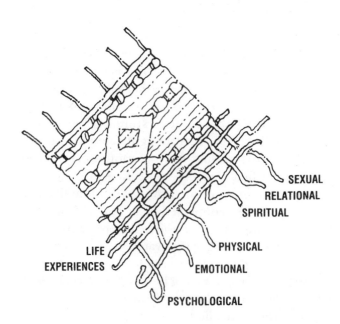

SEXUAL
RELATIONAL
SPIRITUAL
PHYSICAL
LIFE
EXPERIENCES
EMOTIONAL
PSYCHOLOGICAL

You may have identified with some of the stories we have shared, or you may be having different struggles. We hope that by the end of this chapter you will have a clear picture of the places in your life that need healing and renewal. We encourage you to make notes in a journal or in this book about your thoughts, ideas, or questions. You may have concentrated so hard in the past on controlling your feelings about your abortion that you never realized how some of your current struggles began or escalated because of the abortion.

PSYCHOLOGICAL STRUGGLES

Let's begin by discussing self-esteem. You made your abortion decision with a certain sense of self-worth. Think back now about that value and esteem.

- How did you feel about yourself before you got pregnant?
- Since your abortion, how have you thought of yourself?
- Has your sense of self-worth declined?
- On a scale of 1–10 locate your self-esteem before you got pregnant, at the time of your abortion, and now.
- Use several adjectives to describe yourself.
- What does the description tell you about your self-image?

As you made decisions about your pregnancy and abortion, you probably received many different messages. Some of these messages came from your family, the father of the baby, or your friends. Other messages came from inside your own head and heart. Try to recall the things you heard. Realize that not all the messages you received were direct; some things were implied.

- Can you remember any ideas that were implied or influenced by others?
- What do you remember saying to yourself?

• What do you remember others telling you?

These messages have long-lasting effects on your self-esteem. The words ring in your ears and burrow like a termite deep into your psyche long after the abortion decision and procedure are over. Once your self-esteem is wounded, future decisions are based on a distorted view of who you think you are. Add to this your fear of being found out or known for who you "really" are, and you become virtually blocked in your ability to feel loved and valuable to another person.

Our sexuality as women is wounded by abortion because it affects the roles we are expected to fill in society. Many post-abortion women struggle psychologically because their identities as mothers, nurturers, or females have been lost or wounded. This distortion also makes it difficult to find fulfillment in any love relationships.

EMOTIONAL STRUGGLES

The abortion has affected your emotions, specifically your ability to feel. Many women commonly experience swings to one end of the emotional spectrum or the other. On one end of the spectrum, many women cut themselves off from their feelings. They honestly don't know how they feel, or they push their true feelings down because they are afraid to feel. The protective mask they wear in front of other people makes them seem like a "cold fish" at times.

On the other end of the spectrum a woman may experience a constant roller coaster ride of feelings. She may feel everything intensely and personally, even about trivial matters. The emotions that tend to run amok for post-abortion women are strong ones: fear, anger, depression, and loneliness. Strong emotions also tend to explode at inappropriate times, making relationships more difficult.

The bottom line is that whether our emotions are unexpressed or indiscriminately expressed, they cause problems. A woman uses all of her energy in trying to control or hide her feelings. This leaves little energy for engaging life on any other level.

Examine your own emotional reactions.

- Can you describe your feelings about the abortion?
- How do you deal with your emotions in general?
- How would significant others in your life describe you emotionally?

PHYSICAL STRUGGLES

We have seen women at our counseling centers who have been physically damaged because of complications following their abortion. These problems range from minor infection to infertility. We have also seen women experiencing physical symptoms that are not physiologically induced. Many studies have linked emotional stress and illness: Headaches, back pain, frequent colds, and asthma are just a few ailments that have been closely linked to buried emotions and stress. Professionals have acknowledged that sickness can have a physical cause or be symbolic of emotional distress.

When a woman chooses to medicate her pain with drugs or alcohol, her abortion may be the cause. Victoria, whom you'll hear more about later, drank continually from Thanksgiving to Christmas every year—without knowing why. It took her more than twelve years to consciously remember that, while in college, she had an abortion right before Thanksgiving and stoically went home for Christmas as if nothing had ever happened. She purposefully forgot the event, but her feelings refused to be forgotten. She tried to ignore them, and when they began to surface, she fought to suppress them with alcohol.

Many women we see also struggle with eating disorders. In addition to being an expression of self-hatred, anorexia and bulimia can alter moods and emotions just as alcohol or drugs would. Alcohol and drug abuse, as well as eating disorders, can cause serious physical damage sometimes to the point of death.

Some women have considered suicide—the ultimate physical abuse. When a woman wants to kill herself, she may be saying, "I don't deserve to live." This woman does not feel that her life is valuable or maybe she just wants to end her pain and conflict. Very likely she is trying to retreat from many painful feelings, particularly grief, anger, or shame. But, suicide is not a proper expression of these feelings.

What about you?

- Do you have specific physical problems that you think could be related to your abortion?
- Are you engaged in any behavior that puts your physical health at high risk?
- What is your relationship with/dependency on drugs? Alcohol? Abusive relationships? Avoiding annual checkups? Eating disorders? Suicidal behavior?
- Do you think your stress or emotions are expressing themselves through a physical ailment?

If any of these physical struggles are yours, you would be wise to make an appointment with your doctor, as well as with a counselor. We urge you to not let your physical problems continue unchecked.

SPIRITUAL STRUGGLES

All people are spiritual beings and have spiritual needs. They were made to seek after and live in relationship with One higher than themselves. They all need help from that Someone, and they all need to be "connected" with that Power. We believe that Power is God and that human fulfillment is not possible apart from a relationship with Him.

Virtually all of the women we counsel raise questions about their spiritual nature. Although these women come from diverse spiritual backgrounds, we have noted that their concerns fall into two broad categories.

The first category raises a group of questions centered around an individual relationship with God. Consider your answers to the following:

- Is there a God? If so, who is God?
- What is He like? What are His character traits?
- What does it mean to have a relationship with God?
- What degree of personal interaction can you have with Him?
- How would you describe your relationship with God?
- How do you reflect this relationship in your life?
- Has your relationship with God changed since your abortion?
- If so, can you determine the reasons?
- How do you think God feels about your pregnancy and your abortion?
- Did you have any interaction with God while you were deciding about your abortion?
- How do you feel toward God in relation to your abortion: angry, abandoned, confused, afraid?

We have generally seen women who either distance themselves from God or actively pursue God as a response to their abortion. One way cuts off your spiritual nature; the other way attempts to understand and reconcile the spiritual nature into everyday life.

The second category of spiritual concerns our clients look at involves their interaction with the religious community. No matter what religious system you grew up in, your background influenced many of your ideas and feelings. These messages play a part in your self-concept and your decision-making.

- Can you identify the basis of your belief system?

- What is your religious community's stance on abortion?
- How do they react to the issue or to a woman who has had an abortion?
- Do you feel you must hide your abortion and your feelings?
- Has your grief been discounted or trivialized?
- Have you been wounded by a church, its teachings, or its people?

RELATIONAL STRUGGLES

The trauma of abortion deals severe blows to a woman's relationships. She may have lasting problems with trust, intimacy, or setting and honoring boundaries. Without a healthy understanding of what these concepts are, much less a positive experience in each area, a woman cannot maintain successful relationships.

First, *trust* is essential to a healthy relationship. When we trust someone to treat us with respect and concern, we are able to share our true selves with them.

- To whom can you tell your secrets?
- Who will be concerned about your well-being?
- Who will help you work through your personal struggles?

Nancy didn't trust anyone. Her boyfriend, Joey, left her soon after the pregnancy was ended; she felt her parents had never cared for her. Thus, the people she thought she could trust were not there when she needed them. Her heart believed it was too great a risk to trust anyone else.

Another client, Sarah, told everyone she met about her abortion in an attempt to see if they could be trusted. Sarah believed that if people knew about the abortion they wouldn't like her, so she tested them. Would they still like her if they knew her worst secret?

Second, *intimacy* involves being connected to another person on a level that is deeper than the surface. Knowing another person and being known deeply by them is characteristic of an intimate relationship. When you have intimacy in your relationship, the other person fully accepts you "as is." They don't expect you to perform in order to earn their love and acceptance; that is conditional love and it does not create intimacy. A willingness to be open and honest are qualities that help you to be intimate with others.

Many women become confused when evaluating the level of intimacy they have in their relationships. Sexual involvement, the quantity of time spent with another person, and longing for intimacy may lead them to believe they have intimacy, when in fact they may not. If your relationships are characterized by a lack of communication, the holding back of your emotions, and conditional love, you probably are not experiencing true intimacy.

Setting and maintaining healthy boundaries is the third ingredient for maintaining healthy relationships. Setting boundaries means putting up the right kind of fences, the kind that protects and gives definition to relationships. The goal is to have "healthy" boundaries—a solid fence with a gate. You must decide which people to let inside the gate and which ones to keep at a distance on the other side of the fence. Common examples of inappropriate boundaries include physically and emotionally abusive relationships, always giving in to another's preferences, or getting sexually involved with someone too quickly.

Appropriate boundaries in relationships include getting to know a person well and taking the time to find out about their past, what they struggle with, what their intentions and habits are. You know you have good boundaries when you feel safe in a relationship, when you can negotiate to get your needs met, when the other person respects and honors your ideas, feelings, and commitments.

Relationships with men are particularly difficult for a woman who has had an abortion. Many times the man she trusted violated her boundaries, betrayed her trust, and broke an intimate bond with her. She then has difficulty with establishing good relationships with any other men as a result.

The number of books on the market dealing with male/female relationships is a testament to our society's desire to improve our relationships. In Appendix E you will find some references for further reading if you would like to take a deeper look at relationship issues.

SEXUAL STRUGGLES

Developing a healthy sexual identity is a challenge for every individual. Many women find this struggle even harder after their abortion experience. When women receive conflicting messages about sexuality, abortions may magnify these conflicts.

Some women chose to deal with their sexual struggles following abortion by pretending to be nonsexual. They feel that their sexuality propelled them into becoming pregnant and getting an abortion. So they feel it is safer to cut off their sexuality rather than to risk another pregnancy. Often they hide their sexuality by consciously or unconsciously wearing plain clothes, gaining weight, or dropping out of the social scene.

Other women struggle because they feel sexually vulnerable when they become over-involved in their relationships. Monique decided that her main problem was getting too emotionally involved. She would remind herself to "keep it light and easy," meaning no commitments, no pain. After a couple of years filled with a series of short-term sexual relationships, Monique felt like an object. What she really wanted was to feel valued. Monique's sexual lifestyle choices only made her feel more empty instead of safe.

Examine your own sexual struggles:

- What does it mean to be female?
- How should I express my femininity? How should I express my sexuality?
- Is there a difference between sex and sexuality?
- What kind of a sexual lifestyle do I want?
- What are my "rights" as a woman?
- What is the value I place on physical attractiveness, motherhood, and having a career?

Along with these questions, other concerns come up in counseling for some of our clients. They have fears about infertility, birth control, sharing their sexual past with a marriage partner, talking with children about their sexuality and lifestyle.

One of the most difficult issues we encounter in counseling is past sexual abuse. An abortion and its companion problems may trigger emotions and unresolved grief related to the past. Childhood or sexual abuse may have made a woman more vulnerable as an adult. We never take these issues lightly, and we encourage you to seek a professional or a group that can help you work through any memories you may have of childhood abuse whether sexual, physical, or emotional. You deserve to break the cycle of victimization, for your own well-being and for the health of your relationships.

HEALTHY RELATIONSHIPS AND SIGNIFICANCE

We believe that your abortion experience probably blocks certain areas of your life and keeps you from freely giving or receiving the treasures of a fulfilled, healthy relationship and from having a sense of significance.

Relationships

Humans need relationships. After all, psychologists tell us that most emotional diseases are caused by breaks in relationships. Neglect, abuse, abandonment, and dysfunctional families all have at their root unmet basic needs, the two deepest needs being healthy relationships and a sense of significance. Despite the world's imperfections, it is possible to reach our full potential and live healthy, productive lives when these needs are met.

Healthy relationships embody affection, affirmation, companionship, giving, receiving, sharing, physical touching, and nurturing. In good relationships, a woman loves someone and is loved in return. Receiving love sets her feet firmly on solid ground, surrounding her with the security she needs in order to move out into the world. A sense of love is thus an essential ingredient for survival. It gives a woman a place of refuge, a place warm and safe, a place to renew her bruised self when the world is cruel. Loving others is the other side of healthy relationships. She becomes a nurturer when she loves someone.

- How would you describe your relationships?
- Have you been trying to survive without loving, secure relationships?

Significance

Humans spend a large measure of their time involved in a search for significance. Every human being has been designed by God with great value, as well as a unique purpose to fulfill. This value and purpose give a sense of significance to life. Words which describe human value are *innate, priceless, God-given, inherent.* This value does not hinge on productivity, material possessions, other people's opinions, race, physical condition, developmental stage, state of mind, religion, or any of the other ten thousand means people use to devalue others. Knowing her value gives a woman self-esteem, self-worth, a sense of individuality. You are human; therefore, you are valuable.

- How does that last statement make you feel?

- What makes you unique?
- What do you believe gives value to your life?

Knowing her value also motivates a woman to fulfill her unique purpose in the world because she has direction in life. Every element, plant, and animal in nature has a job to do that makes the whole world work. Each part of our bodies has a unique purpose: The nose smells; the eyes see; each muscle does a different job. Each human being is part of a larger body or community, if you will, and is uniquely gifted to contribute to that community for the good of the whole.

- Have you ever considered what your unique purpose and contribution might be?
- What are your strengths?

Self Assessment

We have designed a short self-assessment questionnaire to help you to examine your post-abortion feelings and to pinpoint where you may be blocked in feelings of self-worth and your relationships.

1. Do you often struggle with any feelings connected to your abortion? Yes____ No____ Can you name any of these feelings?_____
_____
_____

2. Are you able to talk about abortion in general or about your own abortion? Never___When it seems appropriate___ All the time____

3. When sharing about your abortion, are you overwhelmed by feelings? Yes____ No____

4. Do you often feel so depressed that you cannot maintain your normal routine? Yes____ No____

5.   Are there certain times during the year when you find yourself more depressed, sick, or accident-prone? Yes____ No____ When?_____

_____

_____

6.   Do you feel your personality has changed since your abortion? Yes____ No____ If yes, please use three adjectives to describe yourself:

Before your abortion	After your abortion
_____	_____
_____	_____
_____	_____

7.   Below are some thoughts that many post-abortion women have. Please check any messages that sound familiar to you or that you find yourself repeating over and over:
    ____I don't want to talk or think about it.
    ____If there is a God, why did this happen?
    ____I hate.
    ____I'm really sorry.
    ____If I just concentrate on something else, this will
       all go away.
    ____Nothing matters anymore.
    ____I'll never get over this.
    ____I had to do it. I didn't have any other choices.

8.   Do you often experience nightmares, flashbacks, or hallucinations that might be related to your abortion? Yes__ No____

9.   Do you avoid persons or situations that could possibly trigger abortion-related memories and emotions? Yes____ No____ Who are these people or what are those situations?

_____

_____

10.   If you do not have any children, do you fear that you may be infertile? Yes____ No____ If you have children, do you experience intense anxiety about their safety? Yes____ No____ About your ability to parent? Yes____ No____

11.   Has your use of drugs or alcohol increased since your abortion? Yes_____ No_____

12.   Do you engage in any of the following self-destructive behaviors?
_____eating disorders
_____abusive relationships
_____increased unprotected sexual activity

13.   Do you often have any of the following thoughts?
_____I hate myself.
_____I don't want to live anymore.
_____I don't belong here.
_____I just can't do this any longer.
_____The world would be better off without me.
_____My life isn't worth anything.
_____If I weren't around, that would show them. They'd be
       sorry then.

14.   Do you ever think about hurting yourself? Yes_____
No_____ Have you ever made a suicide plan? Yes_____
No_____

Special note: If you answer yes to questions 11, 12, 13, or 14, please find a therapist whom you feel safe with and who can help you learn how to protect yourself. You will find a list of some helpful contacts in the Appendix or you can call your local crisis hot line. Talking with someone in your area can help you work through any desperate feelings you may be having.

We hope you have identified some of your personal wounds and what needs of yours are not being met. We also hope you feel some relief in knowing that there is a reason for your struggles. In the next section of the book we will help you walk through a healthy grieving process and find the hope waiting for you in a life free from your past pain.

PART TWO

❦

The Road

to

Wholeness

CHAPTER FOUR

The Healing Process

Whether it's a broken bone, a tumor, a heart attack, a minor cut, or a broken heart, healing takes time. Pain is unavoidable any time you touch an open cut or a haunting memory.

The emotional healing that is a part of grief work is the same as physical healing. It takes time and you must trust that the process and treatment will work. As you begin the healing process, you may need to adjust to new information. You will need to learn how to protect yourself from further injury and to use your energy to make positive changes in your life, just as you might have to change some aspects about your life after a heart attack.

The process of emotional healing is like cleaning out the wounds a child suffers when he or she falls. Someone who cares for and is trusted by the child must evaluate the damage and apply the right salve. The healing balm may be smelly and even sting at first; however, the balm soon begins to soothe the wound. In time the pain lessens and the wound does heal. One of our clients said it well: "It's taken a while, but I now have other feelings besides my pain." Another client said, "I no longer feel like I have a gaping hole in my heart."

Those of you touched by abortion have very significant losses. The list may include the child, the relationship with the father of the baby, innocence, the experience of motherhood, and a sense of control. If a woman has not grieved these losses, she still carries within her the wounds they have caused—wounds that need healing.

Many professionals call this healing process "grief work" or "working through grief issues." The operative word here is *work*. We wish we could tell you that it will be easy, but grieving is hard work. It takes time and energy and, most often, involves others to help with the work. However those who work hard are rewarded well, as many of our clients will gladly tell you: "It got easier as I went along." "I got stronger and I wasn't alone in the harder places." "This has been the most rewarding work I've ever done."

What does that work involve? The healing work for Post-Abortion Stress involves grieving the long-buried or denied losses surrounding your abortion. As we discussed in Chapter 3, unresolved grief affects many areas of your life, blocking your ability to fully enter healthy relationships. You are also unable to reach your full potential if you've closed off areas of your life. Healing hurts and integrating the losses experienced as a result of abortion will enable you to move forward in a positive way. It will also help you to find ways to fulfill your previously unmet needs.

WHAT IS GRIEVING?

Grief is the emotional suffering experienced following the loss of anyone or anything that is important. This emotional suffering most often causes deep sorrow. In *A Tearful Celebration*, J. E. Means describes grief in this way:

> In great grief, the deep, inner springs of the soul are clogged with very intense feelings, often so jumbled as to be impossible to sort out. There is a sense of overwhelming sadness. . . . The permanency and totality of separation produce an ache beyond description. . . . There seems to be no path out of the maze of lostness and depression. Every passage seem[s] closed, every light seem[s] extinguished, and every hope seem[s] futile.[1]

Many different sensations accompany grief: a sinking feeling in the pit of the stomach, a hole that can't be filled, a cold and trembling feeling, empty arms that ache, a sense of being weighted down, or an intense feeling of depression or loneliness. Some of the common responses to grief are a lack of concentration, motivation, or energy; a disruption in eating or sleeping habits; depression that just won't go away; or being too emotionally overwhelmed to function.

Grief is a long and personal experience for each individual. Different factors affect how each person responds to loss. Society's reaction to the loss, an individual's own mixed feelings, the ability to handle emotional pain, and the lack of personal awareness of loss can all cause grief to take an unhealthy turn.

As a whole, our society has little patience with people who are grieving. There is an unrealistic expectation that no matter how great the loss, the grieving one should quickly "get over it" and return to life again as though nothing significant has happened. In the case of an abortion, many people don't recognize that there has been a loss and, therefore, don't understand the need to grieve. These attitudes create a climate which makes grieving in a healthy way very difficult.

Abortion also causes ambivalence about the nature of the losses. A woman may have mixed feelings about the pregnancy, the loss of the baby, and the relationship with the father. These conflicting feelings make grieving a difficult task.

An individual's ability to tolerate different levels of emotional pain may interrupt or slow the process of grief. Medicating with drugs or alcohol will also interfere with grieving.

Another obstacle that may interfere with grieving is not really knowing what it is that you have lost. That a person, the aborted baby, has died may become more obvious to someone who has suffered an abortion, but what of some of the more nebulous losses? Abortion has also cost a woman the loss of her dreams of motherhood, of her decision-making power, or her self-confidence.

Grieving has no magic formula, for there is no proper way to grieve. You will have to recognize your loss and grieve in your own way and in your own time. In the midst of grieving, you may often find yourself confused about your feelings, purpose, values, direction, and desire. At times you may feel that you cannot see the light at the end of the tunnel; but, although the emotional turmoil may be staggering, it does not have to defeat you. Working through your grief will restore your hope, cause you to take a deeper look into your soul, and enable you to live a life of love, value, and purpose—perhaps for the first time.

HEALING STEPS TO POST-ABORTION RECOVERY

By now you may be asking: How do I get from where I am now to where the hope, love, and purpose is? We hear this question from women in many ways: "Okay, so I need to grieve. But how?" "I've been talking, crying, feeling, and saying 'I'm sorry' for a long time. Why does it all keep coming back?" "What do I need to do to feel better?"

These are the first questions that virtually every client asks when she is ready to begin the healing process. We have outlined below healing steps in the grief process. Although the steps in the process often overlap or do not happen in sequence, each step has some unique characteristics. It's normal for someone who is grieving to flip back and forth between the steps or stages of grief. However, each tiny step will move you further out of your pain.

Steps to Healing

1. *Step out of the dark.* Denying that abortion has affected my life is no longer a legitimate coping mechanism. I must begin to deal with the reality of my abortion experience. I can live with the truth and the loss, no

matter how painful. I can accept that my abortion has affected my life. (Chapter 5)

2. *Recognize my real feelings and my real losses.* I need to recognize the feelings I have about my abortion. I will begin grieving by naming the losses I have suffered as a result of my abortion. This will begin the process of burying my past and opening my life fully to the present. (Chapter 6)

3. *Cancel my empty deals.* Using bargaining and other coping mechanisms is the way that I have made deals with myself so I could bury my feelings. These empty deals are the things I have done to make the pain go away. I will learn to recognize the deals I've made and cancel them. (Chapter 7)

4. *Unlock the trapdoor of guilt and shame.* Shame has locked me in a prison and makes it impossible for me to heal. Shame is the unhealthy emotion that tells me I am not a worthwhile person—that I am bad. Guilt is a healthy emotion that lets me know I have stepped outside my boundaries. I will choose not to live under shame, and I will learn to live within healthy boundaries. (Chapter 8)

5. *Take the lid off.* My post-abortion anger is a pressure cooker that gives me the illusion of power and hides my deeper pain. I will learn to express my angry feelings in a constructive way, so that I don't explode. I will also uncover and deal with the deeper pain that lies beneath my anger. (Chapter 9)

6. *Do not surrender to my depression but work through it.* Long-term depression over my abortion robs me of the ability to live a healthy, productive life. Depression consumes all of my energy. I can learn not to surrender to crippling depression. (Chapter 10)

7. *Find freedom in forgiveness.* I will learn how to forgive myself and others, so that I can break the chains of bondage to my past. Offering and receiving forgiveness frees me to walk into a new life. (Chapter 11)

8. *Become reconciled.* I have grieved my abortion losses and taken back my life. I can now focus my attention on the present, by reclaiming the inner beauty God has given me through unconditional self-acceptance and love. (Chapter 12)

Remember that healing is a process. It does not happen instantaneously, and it does not always follow a straight line. Expect the movement to be up and down, in and out, much like a hilly backroad. The places of major movement and rest are different for everyone. Since you are unique in every way, your grieving will be unique as well.

Also remember to take care of yourself while you move along at your own pace. Be totally honest, and trust yourself to acknowledge your secrets. Explore and experience all of your feelings; they will only overwhelm you if you refuse to deal with them. If handling your emotions becomes hard, slow down or reach out to someone you can trust with your feelings and your story, and most importantly, someone who will validate your grieving process. This could be an individual or a group who understands and will encourage you as you work through the grief issues in your life.

If you want a therapist, Appendix D lists some places to use for a referral. If you struggle with alcohol or drug problems or an eating disorder, it is important to seek help because these issues will hamper your grieving. And if you have any suicidal thoughts, please call someone you can trust; do not try to proceed on your own.

Now we are ready to move to the first step in grief work, stepping out of the dark. As you begin the process, you may be encouraged to read this letter from someone who was once where you are—but who now stands in the light:

My dear friends,

It has been almost a year since I first met my post-abortion group. Over the course of those group meetings, I had many questions. I used to wonder what other women had gone through with their abortion experiences—and how they had been healed afterwards . . . and what *healed them. Or why some women didn't seem to need healing . . . Were they really as okay as they seemed? Did they go home and secretly cry every night and struggle with the same pain I did? Exactly how would someone come to the point of trusting God to take away their remorse?*

I wanted to write this letter to champion each one of you very brave women and to let you know that God has drawn you to this place only to love you and free you from the past! I know this because He did that for me and I continue to be increasingly thankful for His mighty power that totally heals hurts. Nothing else here on earth I've seen can do that.

Two weeks after my abortion I became very depressed and could hardly function at work. I had terrible nightmares every night. One night I begged God to show me a glimmer of mercy. A few days later I mustered the courage to approach a friend and after three straight hours of crying and spilling my guts, he told me that God loved me and that he would stand by me. The next day my friend made a contact with a counselor for me. I went to see her and soon started the post-abortion group.

And there I was in this odd place with these other women—my heart twisted up in a knot of shame and anger—realizing finally that I was not the first woman in history to have an abortion, determined to ask God for a second chance, and ready to grieve for my lost baby.

As I sought to know the truth, God let me see it. And it was very painful—my abortion did end a life . . . , my lifestyle that led up to it was crippled and wayward . . . , the consequences are not pretty . . . , but the pain of accepting those realities keeps turning out to be my friend.

So I want to tell you to seek the truth and the truth will set you free. The truth does set us free! Keep going!

I encourage you because I know that it is hard. I encourage you because I know that you may feel "why even try," "I'm scum," or "I have to do something big to make up for this" . . . but those are just passing feelings. I especially encourage you not to give up–and don't listen to anyone who tries to hinder your progress.

Take courage as you allow God to change your heart. God will give you the strength you need to continue . . . and you will experience God's faithfulness, every single time you look for it. . . . His promises are reliable every day.

I am so excited as I write this letter because I know that there will soon be great joy in your heart and miracles in your life.

CHAPTER FIVE

Step Out of the Dark

Healing Step 1: Denying that abortion has affected my life is no longer a legitimate coping mechanism. I must begin to deal with the reality of my abortion experience. I can live with the truth and the loss, no matter how painful. I can accept that my abortion has affected my life.

Both Renee and her mom felt a flood of relief as they closed the clinic door behind them. It was over. Now they could close this chapter in their lives. Mom treated Renee to a nice lunch, during which they carefully avoided discussion about the abortion. Renee rested for the next two days. Her dad and sister also felt relieved that this experience was over and done with.

Relief is usually the first feeling women have when leaving the abortion clinic or hospital. Many think, "Whew, no more decisions to make. It's over. I can get on with my life." They believe their feelings of anxiety and fear are over, just as the abortion promised to lift the burden of an unwanted pregnancy.

This relief may last for a matter of hours, days, or months, but no matter how glad you are to have the abortion behind you, that probably isn't the end of it. Regardless of how hard you may try, relief is not a stage that lasts forever.

Most women move straight from relief into denial, either consciously or unconsciously. Denial is okay initially, since you may not be quite ready yet to handle your feelings, but denial is not an effective long-term way to handle your loss. Renee and her family moved quickly into denial believing that they could go on with their lives as if the pregnancy and abortion had never happened. But denial helps you build a distorted reality, regardless of your feelings, as you ignore your loss and your need to grieve. In the long run, denial causes a breakdown in your ability to be honest with yourself and others. This makes it difficult for you to have intimate relationships.

Denying reality, whether it is your feelings or an experience, is like building a protective shell around yourself. Everyone builds a shell to some extent when tragedy strikes, and for a while that shell is a healthy response to shield yourself from unexpected pain. Denial helps suppress emotions about the event that hurt you. However, denial is only meant to last for a short time while your system prepares itself to deal with its pain. Denial is not meant to be a long-term way to cope with our feelings.

When denial is used to suppress a specific hurt for a long time, it becomes a familiar way to deal with other painful incidents. Eventually the covered, suppressed pain and emotions will surface in an attempt to be recognized. This may happen in any area of your life: physical, emotional, spiritual, or relational.

Many women who use denial to deal with their abortion stay in denial about the effects of the abortion too long and build their protective shell too thick. For example, some women wrap themselves in the safe cocoon of a busy life, or they may avoid contact with others by isolating themselves. These lifestyles push back the pain and help a woman stay in denial.

Lynn used denial to cope with her feelings. She scheduled her abortion for Friday afternoon, so she could rest over the weekend and return to work in a high-powered advertising firm on Monday. When Lynn's feelings of sadness or regret tried to surface, Lynn forced herself not to think about the experience. If those feelings did break through, she would tell herself, "It was the right thing for me. It was my choice. I could not pursue my career and be a proper mother." These statements, of course, fed her denial. In addition to her job, she began pursuing her graduate degree, exercised almost every day, and kept her social calendar full. She had lots of dates, but she never saw any one man more than three times.

When another single woman in her office got pregnant and decided to carry her baby, Lynn felt sorry for her. Lynn believed that this woman's promising career would die and that she and her child were destined to be financially strapped. Lynn squelched thoughts of her own pregnancy as she watched the coworker: She made plans that would conflict with the baby shower, and she avoided contact with the new mother as much as possible. When the other woman continued in her career after her baby was born, Lynn ignored every little twinge that said, "Maybe you could have done that, too." Lynn's shell became thicker as she pushed the pain deeper, unconsciously believing, as do many others, that she could live in denial forever.

When Lynn went for her yearly gynecology checkup and pap smear, the nurse did the usual file update. When asked about any previous pregnancies, she flatly stated, "No." Ob-gyns report that many of their patients, when filling out information forms or answering questions, do not reveal past abortions. Women tell themselves, and may really believe, that it was not a pregnancy.

Not only do women deny the pregnancy and abortion experience, but if they do seek help from a therapist, the counselor often does not understand the reality of Post-Abortion Stress. Since her therapist could not validate her feelings as legitimate, the messages Monique received from him intensified her pain and added to her I-am-really-crazy feelings. You may have seen one or more qualified therapists who reinforced your belief that your abortion has nothing to do with your current struggle or "diagnosis," if you have told them about your abortion at all. Pushing your pain and questions aside will not make them go away. The problem is that unresolved feelings and loss concerning your abortion will most likely continue to bother you.

BREAKING DENIAL

Although denial is a very legitimate survival mechanism, an effective way of coping for the moment, you must not stay in denial. Breaking out of denial is essential to healing and growth. However, breaking out of denial is difficult because if no one knows about your abortion, it's easier to stay in denial and keep it a secret. The process of coming out of denial can be very scary. As C.S. Lewis observed: "It's hard to feel because it's something I can't control."[1] At times the emotions and sense of loss will threaten to overwhelm, possibly even destroy, your life. You may fear that the process will leave you unable to function.

We understand that fear. But the post-abortion healing process can only begin when a woman faces the reality that her abortion has impacted her life. Facing reality is tough: "I chose to have an abortion." "When I made my decision I was in a state of crisis and under lots of pressure." "This abortion has affected my life." "This abortion may have affected the lives of my loved ones." "There are feelings I have pushed down." "I have experienced the loss of a child."

INFLUENCES ON YOUR DECISION

Early in their counseling Monique, Nancy, Renee, and most other women looked at the decision-making process that led them to choose an abortion. Often how past circumstances affected your decision making is not clear. These past circumstances may even continue to affect your responses to your abortion today.

Take a moment to reflect on your past circumstances.

- What choices did you feel you had?

• Who and what influenced those choices?

Several factors helped shape your decision to abort. Your decision was heavily influenced by your circumstances, your resources, your emotions, and the messages you received from others. Rarely do we make a decision based on only one of these sets of factors. Certain factors may have been more intense than others; however, it is common for your reasons to overlap. Let's look at the four factors in the illustration.

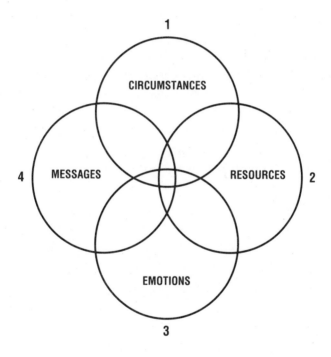

Circle 1 represents circumstances. This may include your family situation, your income level, your job or school security, your age, your health at the time of your pregnancy, and your relationship with the father of your baby. Renee's decision to get an abortion was greatly influenced by her circumstances, specifically her parents' feelings and her desire to go to college. Monique's decision had been based on her relationship with Peter, as well as the fact that she was already a single mother of two.

- What were your circumstances at the time of your abortion decision?
- What circumstance most affected your decision?

Circle 2 represents the resources that were or were not available to you at the time of your decision. For example, many young women find themselves pregnant without insurance, and low-income health care is not always readily available. In looking toward a future with a child, living arrangements, a secure and decent income, and quality child care must be considered. Especially important to single mothers is a support system that they can rely on for the many emotional and practical needs that arise.

- Did any of these concerns cross your mind when you found out you were pregnant?
- Which ones worried you the most?

Most of the decisions made in crisis are full of emotions, which is represented by circle 3. Your emotional state at the time you decided to abort is critical for two reasons: Emotionally you perceived your pregnancy as an unexpected complication, and hormones were likely wreaking havoc on your body. Thus, an important choice was made even more difficult.

- Try to remember how you felt at that time. Did you worry a lot? Did you feel stressed out or like you were being pulled apart? Did you cry often? Were you in shock about what was happening to you?
- How did you cope with the physical changes in your body?

You were also influenced by messages, represented by circle 4. Messages can be external, from friends, family, and society. A direct verbal message can sometimes be blatantly obvious: Peter gave Monique a very clear message to get an abortion; Renee's father told her outright that she must abort. The message Renee received from her mother was harder to discern: Although Mom's verbal message was unclear, she supported the abortion by taking Renee to the clinic and not talking with Renee about her feelings. In contrast, Nancy's influence came from a lifetime of what she perceived to be indirect messages from her parents that said, "You're no good." "We don't value you." "Don't disappoint us again."

Internal messages, those thoughts and tiny voices inside your head, are used as filters to structure and manage your life. Monique told herself that she shouldn't have gotten pregnant, that she couldn't manage with three children. Nancy had no trouble convincing herself that she was such a failure that she couldn't possibly make a good life for herself, let alone her baby. Renee kept telling herself it was better for her to abort so she could achieve her college and career goals.

Examine the messages in your own life regarding your abortion.

- What verbal and nonverbal messages helped shape your decision?
- What did your family say? What did your family not say?
- How did your friends react? What did they think about your options?
- Did you consider the opinions of people from your church, roommates, boyfriend, or husband?
- What message did society give you?
- What messages did your internal voice tell you?

Probably factors in all four circles led you to make your decision. Can you determine some of these things that may still be influencing how you make decisions today?

LOOKING BACK

Joanne had a hard time breaking her denial. When she was thirty, the last of three children started school and she was excited about finishing her degree and having a career. Although she thought it important to be home with them until they started school, she felt smothered, trapped by motherhood.

Her husband ran a thriving business, and they had a busy social life with his clients. But he was not home much, and it had been a long time since Joanne had felt any genuine love from her husband. Sometimes they would have an intimate evening, and she would hope for a deeper relationship. The next morning, however, she would cry in her pillow after he left for work, feeling that the night had really meant nothing to him.

Then Joanne discovered she was pregnant again. Together she and her husband decided abortion was the best choice. They drove to another city so no one would know, got through the procedure, and drove home without speaking to each other.

Life went on as usual, but Joanne noticed her husband becoming even more distant from her and the family. She finished her degree and almost never thought about the abortion again. She had affairs with two men who paid some attention to her, and she and her husband eventually divorced. Temporarily, Joanne was devastated, but she went on.

She found a job in another city, where she met and married a fine man named Jim. He was a deeply spiritual man and loved her unconditionally. She felt much stronger in this relationship than she ever had. The church they attended talked a lot about abortion, which was difficult for Joanne. For several years she unconsciously avoided any contact with the issue or the "pro-life" people. Joanne thought that if anyone in church knew she had had an abortion she would be treated like a second-class citizen. So she pretended it never happened.

But as Joanne got to know the people in this church, some of the women talked about their past abortions. A vague uneasiness set in; Joanne had come to believe that God forgave her, but she began to wonder if that abortion had affected her life after all.

She and Jim agreed that she should talk with a reputable counselor who had experience with Post-Abortion Stress. The counselor opened the session with a list of questions she felt would help Joanne explore whether she was in denial about any of her abortion experience.

They didn't get through all the questions during that first visit because the counselor knew it was important for Joanne to go at her own speed. Sometimes Joanne could answer several questions quickly, as if the answers had been inside her for a long time; others she took home to ponder and discuss later. Over time she realized that her nagging uneasiness came from her profound loss over aborting a child she could have loved.

Are you in denial about the effect your abortion has had on your life? The questions which follow are similar to the ones Joanne worked through. We know these are difficult questions. The process of breaking denial is hard. The truth has been buried so long, and tough truths about yourself are always hard to face.

You may need to talk with someone about each one and ask questions. This is a big step so take the time to write in a journal your feelings and thoughts as they come. Take courage in the fact that this is the first step toward healing and wholeness.

Are You in Denial About the Impact of Abortion in Your Life?

1. Was there a moment before (or after) the abortion when you wondered if you made the right choice?

2. What caused the most pressure as you decided whether or not to abort?

3. Were you alone during this time?

4. You may have felt you had no choice. What led you to that belief?

5. Did you believe that the abortion would end this chapter in your life? What do you think about that now?

6. What purpose, significance, or meaning did you believe your life had at the time of your abortion? What do you believe now?

7. Was getting on with your life after your abortion difficult? What was the hardest thing for you to do after your abortion?

8. Have you been keeping your abortion a secret? How has keeping this secret affected you? Who are you most intent on keeping the secret from? Do you feel that keeping this secret has cost you anything?

9. Do you feel like you are denying yourself anything because of your abortion? What longings and desires have you denied yourself? What activities have you not allowed yourself to participate in?

10. What are you doing to keep from facing difficult feelings about the abortion?

11. Has anyone in your life supported your denial? How has that affected you? How has that affected them? How has that affected your relationship?

12. What emotions did you avoid in order to go through with your abortion?

13. What emotions have you not allowed to surface since the abortion? What feelings do you try to avoid?

14. What purpose, significance, and meaning did you believe your baby's life had at the time of your abortion? What do you believe now?

At this point it would probably be helpful for you to go back over your answers and make a list of the important issues that you uncovered or revisited as you worked through the questions in this chapter. This will be helpful as you continue. In the next chapter we will be looking more closely at the feelings you have and will help you name the losses you have suffered.

CHAPTER SIX

Recognize Real Feelings and Real Losses

Healing Step 2: I need to recognize the feelings I have about my abortion. I will begin grieving by naming the losses I have suffered as a result of my abortion. This will begin the process of burying my past and opening my life fully to the present.

Counselors have a saying: "Feelings are everywhere, so be gentle." Legitimate, valuable, and vital, feelings make people fully human and fully alive. Feelings motivate actions and responses; many times they are so powerful they can actually control thoughts and behavior.

What you learn early in life about feelings seems to stick with you throughout your life. You may have learned to express your feelings in healthy or not so healthy ways. You may have learned not to express certain emotions, or to express no feelings at all. You may have learned to always be polite, always smile, never cry, or never ever express anger. You may block your feelings simply because you do not know how to stop them from overwhelming you and everything around you.

You may have been the victim of someone else acting on feelings that totally controlled them, and those actions may have wounded you deeply. Anytime feelings are in total control of someone's actions, they have too much influence and that is not healthy. There is a vast difference between allowing yourself to express your feelings appropriately and letting your feelings control your life. Expressing feelings in a way that harms anyone, including yourself, only produces pain.

Many times we see women who have no balance in their emotions and are at one extreme or the other. On one side, some women totally shut down their feelings, never allowing them to surface. On the opposite end, other women express all of their feelings indiscriminately, without regard for themselves or others. For these women, the feelings and the expression of them are all that matters.

Feelings serve us well when combined with clear concise thinking. When the head and the heart work together in the expression of emotions, positive results occur. Learning this balance takes time, commitment, and work, especially when a person must change the early lessons about feelings.

You may be shocked to hear that feelings are good, valid, and vital to a healthy life, but it is true. Your feelings are a valuable and legitimate part of your life. The way you feel about things are neither right or wrong, bad or good—they just are. Acknowledging and appropriately expressing feelings is important. Knowing the reasons behind feelings is also important. Having the ability to feel deeply and allow the energy from your feelings to produce positive action in your life is an invaluable gift.

Even though you may not always know how to balance feelings, consider life with no emotions. The words *numb, paralyzed,* and even *dead* come to mind—and some of you have been attempting to live like that in order to survive. But now we hope you will open yourself up to your feelings. In the chapters to come, we will deal with some of the specific feelings that overwhelm many post-abortion women, such as shame, anger, and depression.

EXPRESS YOUR FEELINGS

So many post-abortion women come to us or to a group having *never* expressed their feelings about their abortion, their baby, or their relationship with the father of the baby. You do not have to hide your emotions any longer. We respect and value you and your feelings.

The list which follows will help you discover your feelings. You may already know what some of them are; most of the women we counsel are surprised at how many feelings they identify with from this list. Examine this list from several perspectives and list them in the appropriate areas in your journal or in this book. Don't judge yourself; just be honest. You will also want to look at any feelings you may be or have been avoiding. Perhaps you were really angry at your parents but felt so guilty about the pregnancy that you could not respond to your anger. Maybe your fear of rejection is keeping you from talking about your loss. List your feelings

- today.
- the day of your abortion and the days that followed.
- toward the father of the baby.
- toward the people who performed the abortion.
- toward the people who encouraged you to have the abortion.
- toward the people who have not supported you in ways you felt you needed.
- toward yourself.

As you acknowledge each feeling and circumstance, you will not have to hide your feelings any longer but can integrate them into your life. This will probably be a painful experience, but remember that your emotions will not harm you unless you ignore them. They will enhance your life as you integrate them.

Feelings List

Abandoned	Agony	Angry
Ashamed	Confident	Content
Defeated	Defensive	Depressed
Despair	Disappointed	Distracted
Empty	Fearful	Free
Grieved	Happy	Helpless
Hopeful	Hopeless	Hostile
Hurt	Lonely	Loved
Numb	Overwhelmed	Peaceful
Pressured	Rage	Rejected
Revengeful	Secure	Sorrowful
Suffering	Trapped	Unloved
Used	Violated	Weary

LOSSES

The losses you have suffered as a result of your abortion started during the time you found out about your pregnancy and made your choices. And you have suffered loss—very real loss.

Experts agree that naming the loss helps in the grieving process. You cannot say good-bye to the unknown or to a child you have not acknowledged. Some post-abortion women can clearly express what they are grieving: the child or maybe the relationship with the father of that baby. However, over and over in counseling we hear women talk about feelings of emptiness that they cannot really describe. Often they can finally identify that vague sense of loss when they look over this loss inventory.

Take your time and mark the losses you feel are real in your life. Some losses may have happened at the time of your abortion; others may have occurred at any time since your abortion. Your emotions may vary greatly, depending on the importance you personally attached to each loss. All losses are real and valid, whether someone else feels it or not.

Loss Inventory for Post-Abortion Stress

Primary Losses

_____ Myself
_____ Your baby
_____ Physical health
_____ A change in your relationship with:
    _____ The father of the baby
    _____ Your parents
    _____ God
    _____ Any others (specify)

Secondary Losses

_____ Self-image
_____ Hopes and dreams (of motherhood, for the baby, of marriage)
_____ Freedom to make your own decisions without pressure
_____ Goals
_____ Innocence
_____ Peace of mind, joy, happiness
_____ Ability to trust
_____ Security (feelings of safety)
_____ Beliefs (about yourself, others, life)
_____ Other (specify)

Losses You Suffered as a Result of Your Coping Behavior

_____ Drinking (specify)
_____ Drugs (specify)
_____ Eating disorders (specify)
_____ Anger (specify)
_____ Depression (specify)
_____ Other (specify)

Further, there may be things you are consciously or unconsciously denying yourself because of the way you feel about yourself or your abortion. Does anything come to mind?

Acknowledging and naming your feelings and losses has taken commitment, hard work, and energy. As you continue to work through the steps of the healing process, we will bring you back to this loss inventory as well as your feelings assessment. This is the beginning of a process. Things will continue to come to mind that you will want to add to your list. Feel free to continue this as long as you need. You have some new information and understanding, and you are taking positive action by working through it.

Because we know how much this process has helped many women, we are glad that you have begun. You may still feel raw and painful. Allow the balm of hope to comfort you.

———————————

Again the blood flows
    stinging my heart once more with
    memory of things I cannot
    change.
The pain and color of your dying
    a loss that left my arms an
    aching emptiness.
The uniqueness—
    my calling card to womanhood,
    a reminder of the place I hold in
    space and time.
The sorrow of barrenness
    the burden of my fear
    never again to bring forth the fragrant
    fruit called child.
Again the tears flow
    washing away anger, longing, lies
    and grief—
        but never never
            the place you were to fill.
                    Penny

CHAPTER SEVEN

Cancel Empty Deals

Healing Step 3: Using bargaining and other coping mechanisms is the way that I have made deals with myself so I could bury my feelings. These empty deals are the things I have done to make the pain go away. I will learn to recognize the deals I've made and cancel them.

The world is full of bargains, deals, and chances. It's great to feel that you got a good deal, that you are smart and lucky, and to share a great bargain with friends. But there is always a flip side—a deal that goes sour, an empty bargain, the blind chance that costs you everything and leaves you frustrated and angry.

Post-abortion women often make bargains. Most of these women entered into their bargains unconsciously, and these deals had little to do with material assets. The stakes were far more valuable than that—emotional well-being and peace of mind.

BARGAINS THAT COST TOO MUCH

Megan made a deal. Her end of the bargain was never to make the mistake of becoming pregnant again. For six months after her abortion, she didn't date. Instead Megan studied hard and saw a lot of movies with her girlfriends.

After she started dating again, she tried to avoid any sexual contact. That worked well until she met Greg.

After Megan and Greg moved in together, she began using two different birth control methods in order to protect herself. She hoped that if she didn't put herself at risk, she would never have to think about her abortion again. Megan bargained with her painful memories. They were supposed to go away. But what did she get in return? A life filled with fear.

Lynn struck a different deal. Her end of the bargain, now that she was married and pregnant, was that she would be the best mom in the world. She studied every book she could find on parenting. After her son was born, Lynn did everything "right." She quit her job, breast-fed her baby, made her own baby food, and never left the baby with anyone—not even grandparents. Her hidden desire was to prove her worthiness as a mother. But no matter what she did, she never felt that she was a good enough mom. The deal was an empty one, and Lynn's anxiety grew steadily worse.

Cathy made a deal as well; her bargaining chip was a cause. About a year after Cathy's abortion, a close friend invited her to a fundraiser for a child welfare program. Cathy wrote a big check that night. Within a month she was volunteering regularly for the program; within six months she was also involved politically. Cathy became consumed with this cause and spent little time doing anything else. "Good works" was her partner in this deal. Her heart wanted to make up for the loss it had suffered. If only her efforts could save enough children, all would be well. But Cathy's empty heart never got filled. The more she poured in, the more it needed.

DEFENSE MECHANISMS

We call this process "bargaining." Bargaining is a defense mechanism used to shield oneself from pain, to get back some feeling of personal power, or to make up for an action or a loss.

Have you played "Let's Make a Deal" in connection with your abortion? Most post-abortion women have, in one way or another, as a way to cope with their emotional struggles. And they use common defense mechanisms—denial, compensation, rationalization, repression, projection, and reaction formation. They make deals.

First, just as *denial* is a normal, healthy, initial response to disaster, people normally try to bargain their way out of pain. But neither denial nor bargains work for very long. Using defenses for too long distorts reality.

Second, many women try *compensation,* or restitution, in an attempt to pay back or cover up the damage. Most women bargain by doing good works, joining a cause, or becoming a "perfect" mom, nurse, teacher, caregiver, or person. Many want to have another child immediately after losing one. A grieving mother does these things in an effort to compensate for the loss or to make restitution.

Third, the defense mechanism of *rationalization* is also a form of bargaining. Rationalization is an attempt to justify a decision or to make it okay through reason, hoping that the pain will go away. A woman may surround herself with messages that tell her the decision was the right one or convince herself that she had no other options.

Fourth, *repression* is a way to cope by totally pushing the event out of consciousness, going much deeper than denial. Many women we have counseled with have blocked details of their abortion experience completely from their minds. It is nearly impossible for them to remember dates, places, people involved, or even the abortion experience itself.

Fifth, in an effort to relieve the pressure and responsibility for the choice to abort, sometimes blame is placed on others. This form of coping is called *projection.* Some spend their lives bearing no responsibility for their actions, blaming someone else entirely for the abortion decision. They paint themselves as totally helpless, hoping to gain acceptance and justification.

Sixth, *reaction formation* is an attempt to justify choices and bury feelings by active involvement in a cause that supports those actions. Someone may choose to make her life purpose carrying the banner for this cause. We have also seen women who refuse to ever get pregnant again; this, too, is a form of reaction formation.

Seventh, another form of bargaining manifests itself in messages you repeatedly tell yourself: "I'll say I'm sorry every day"; "I'll never do this again"; "I'll just try not to think about it." It is as if feelings could be talked into going away. When they don't, there is a never-ending cycle of repeating these messages. You may even use the magical thinking that if you just try harder it will work. But no matter how hard you work at the wrong things, they will never work. The old saying is true: "If I always do what I've always done, I'll always get what I always got."

REASONS BARGAINS FAIL

Bargains don't pan out for many reasons. First, we need to look at the foundation beneath our bargaining. The foundation looks like a three-legged stool. The three legs that hold up the deal or bargain are fear, chance, and fantasy.

The *fear* is based on the desire not to feel any pain, anger, guilt, or helplessness. The problem with this leg is that fear is not stable; it will desert at a moment's notice, leaving the bargainer alone and sinking, without any strength.

The leg of *chance* is not based on a cause-and-effect relationship; it is a roll of the dice. What you want may happen, but more than likely it won't. When you take chances, you don't give any thought to the consequences and rarely discuss your actions with another person. It's a risk, and the cost is usually very high.

The third leg is *fantasy*, or the belief that feelings will go away. You may believe that you didn't suffer loss or that the loss suffered will go away if you bury it deep enough. Fantasy is a way to escape reality. The major fault with fantasy is that when you realistically examine your life, it is still the same as when you left it. Your feelings and losses plague you until you deal with them, even if it takes years.

Any bargain built on this foundation of fear, chance, and fantasy will crumble and fall. Even if you appear stable and secure, you are living on very shaky ground. Think about the bargains you made after your abortion.

BARGAINS WORTH TAKING

Some bets *are* worth taking, however. So how can you make a good deal? First, look at the foundation. A sturdy foundation is built on the solid ground of reality in contrast to fear, chance, and fantasy. Reality is living with the truth—no secrets, no hiding. Truth never changes; truth never uses any disguise to look better. Truth says, "I had an abortion. I have suffered loss and I feel pain as a result of my abortion. I need to grieve." Plant your feet firmly on the foundation of truth. Second, in order to decide if a bargain is worth taking, carefully and clearly investigate the situation. You will want to take a look at all of your options, examining the costs and the benefits of each one. Also, you should seek out any available research or information you may need from trustworthy people, including yourself and God. By approaching your decision-making in this way, you maximize your personal power and choice. Learning to make healthy choices means that you can stop making empty deals that trap you into a constant struggle to run away from or be destroyed by the past.

Cindi, another one of our clients, made a bargain to come to counseling. Initially she figured she would come in and talk, then she would feel better. When Cindi discovered that she didn't feel better instantly and that post-abortion counseling was hard, she quit coming. She didn't want to feel her pain and loss; it was just too costly. Her pattern was to come to a couple of sessions and, when Luci would push her a little, not keep her next few appointments.

Each of the four times Cindi came back to try counseling again, Luci talked with her about the healing process and what the bargain really looked like. Cindi had to make a conscious choice to work at counseling. It took a while, but she now keeps all of her appointments and works hard. Cindi is moving through her pain, not running from it; she canceled her empty bargain.

Linda spent the first few years after her abortion in a series of brief, unhealthy relationships. She began to wonder if she would ever be able to meet someone and be happy. Soon after Linda joined a support group to look at relationship issues, she realized that her inability to trust and feel secure with someone stemmed from her abortion experience. Although it would be tough, Linda knew that in order to have the kind of relationship she wanted, she would have to talk with someone about her abortion and work through her feelings. Linda made this comment about counseling: "When I first heard about post-abortion counseling, I was sure it would never work. After talking with other women, however, I found it was one of the best bargains in town." As she slowly worked through the grief over her abortion and unhealthy relationship choices, she began to see some light at the end of the tunnel. Linda knew she finally had made a good deal.

Exploring the following questions will help you discover the kinds of bargains you have made with yourself. As you lay these empty deals aside and exercise your personal power, you are free to make new and better choices. Your life can be built on the solid foundation of reality.

EMPTY BARGAINS

1. Are you using any defense mechanisms to shield you from your abortion experience? Review the defense mechanisms given in this chapter.
   ____ Compensation
   ____ Rationalization
   ____ Repression
   ____ Projection
   ____ Reaction Formation

2. What bargains do you think you have made?

3. On what foundation is your bargain built?
   What are your fears?
   What chances have you taken?
   What are your fantasies?

4. What were you hoping to gain by making this deal with yourself, your feelings, or someone else?

5. How well has your attempt at bargaining worked? What has it cost you?

6. What concessions or life choices do you feel you have made that were not a good deal at all?

7. What decisions or life choices do you feel you have made that *are* great deals?

As you take a closer look at your life from the perspective of bargaining, you may see some things that need changing. We hope you will begin to lay aside any fears, chances, and fantasies that are keeping your life off-balance. Step down from the stool and plant your feet firmly on the rock of reality. From there you will not be shaken as you continue to grieve.

CHAPTER EIGHT

Unlock the Trapdoor of Guilt and Shame

Healing Step 4: Shame has locked me in a prison and makes it impossible for me to heal. Shame is the unhealthy emotion that tells me I am not a worthwhile person—that I am bad. Guilt is a healthy emotion that lets me know I have stepped outside my boundaries. I will choose not to live under shame and I will learn to live within healthy boundaries.

Susan was seventeen and very shy. She didn't talk much to anybody, especially her parents. Most of the girls she knew had already filled out in ways that obviously attracted boys. She had not developed much and was embarrassed about her very slim body. All the other girls at school seemed to have a knack for the latest hairstyles, fashions, and makeup, but not Susan. She stuck with simple clothes and wore her straight auburn hair in a clean, blunt cut. She had no idea what a natural beauty she was.

Susan's tyrannical dad didn't know what to do with his quiet, demure little girl. He sent her off to the best boarding schools hoping that would "bring her out." Her mom was always busy with civic, social, and volunteer obligations. An only child raised by assorted housekeepers and dorm mothers, Susan felt alone most of her life.

For as long as Susan could remember, her mom nagged her to be more socially active. Most of the time her dad ignored her. He had always wanted a son to take over the business, but that never happened. He was obviously frustrated, and now Susan sometimes wondered if her dad wished she had never been born. She felt ashamed that she wasn't more outgoing . . . and male. How could her parents love a shy, skinny girl they didn't even want?

Susan always tried to be polite, but kept her distance from people. If her parents didn't love her, surely no one else would. She kept her emotions inside and spent a lot of her time alone.

She met Mike at one of her parents' parties. He came with his parents, and he, too, was sort of shy. He went to an all-boys prep school, spent summers traveling with his family, and had little experience with girls.

As they talked, Mike and Susan grew comfortable with each other. They felt a sense of kindred spirits and built a solid friendship over the next year. Both were excited to have someone to attend school and social events with during their senior year. They talked on the phone weekly.

The summer after graduation, the two families took a joint vacation to New England. Mike and Susan loved spending that time together—their one big trip before college. They attended colleges in different states, but they continued to call weekly and to travel to attend social functions together. They decided to take a month-long backpacking trip across Europe the next August. Both sets of parents were pleased that Mike and Susan were interested in life and enjoying each other, and they gladly footed the bill.

By this time, Susan and Mike had definitely fallen in love, so making love on this trip seemed a natural development. Both were inexperienced, but they enjoyed the intimacy. They were too embarrassed to buy condoms, so they did not use any contraceptives.

Susan's cycle had always been unpredictable, so she didn't think anything about it when she missed her period in August, then September. It was mid-October before it occurred to Susan that she could be pregnant. She kept her secret until the week of Thanksgiving when Mike came to take her home for the holidays. She was terrified to tell him. And what about her parents? What would everybody think?

But she knew Mike cared. When they talked, he said he'd gladly marry her, and he would of course go with her to tell her folks. Susan felt better.

They told her parents on the night they arrived home. Susan was shocked at the rage and cursing that came from her dad. Her mother said nothing for a long time; when she finally did, it was to say that they had a doctor friend who could do an abortion. No one would have to know. Mike was ignored, and they both knew he would have no part in the decision.

Susan said, "What about marriage? We love each other."

"You don't know what love is. How could you?" her father retorted.

Her mother said curtly, "What if you marry now and have the baby in May? No one will have any trouble figuring out why. We will not have it. I'll call the doctor tomorrow. I'm sure he can fit you in soon."

Susan's mom scheduled the abortion for the first day of Christmas break. Her folks wouldn't let Mike go with her. Dad dropped her off on his way to work. She trudged into the hospital alone. Tears stung her eyes. How had she gotten into this mess? Couldn't her parents see she and Mike loved each other and wanted to have this baby? But she had hurt them, and she would have to pay. The old shame of not being what her parents wanted washed over her again.

Susan's mom came to pick her up in the early afternoon, and they rode home in silence. Susan went directly to her room, where she stayed most of the weekend. When she came down for dinner, she got a horrible, condemning lecture. Her dad reminded her that he had invested too much in her, sent her to the best schools. How could she be so ungrateful? She was such an embarrassment, he said. Susan just wanted to crawl away and die. And in her heart, she did.

Dad wouldn't let Susan take Mike's phone calls. The family spent the whole Christmas break under the same roof, tense and angry. Susan cried several times a day; she couldn't face Mike after the way her dad acted. She went back to school more withdrawn, insecure, and ashamed than ever.

Mike kept calling and wrote many letters, but Susan couldn't bear to see him. Her parents sent her money, but they rarely called. Finally Mike came to find Susan. The relief of having someone care about her overwhelmed Susan. That summer they eloped, and sparks flew again. This time Dad cut off the only thing he had ever given Susan: money.

Guilt and shame are big motivators of people's behavior. Many are aware of this influence while others unconsciously react or feel pressure to respond in ways they don't understand. Many people spend a lot of time struggling with guilt and shame, not really knowing what they are dealing with or how it is affecting their decisions and their lives. Before coming to counseling, Susan had no idea that shame had played a part in her abortion experience. Her shame and her guilt feelings were indistinguishable and had caused Susan unrelenting pain most of her life.

We believe that there is a vast difference between guilt and shame. Guilt is an emotion you feel when your conscience has been pricked by an action you've taken that falls outside your value system. Your response is, "I made a mistake." Shame is more a state of being, resulting from a lifetime of other people telling you that you are no good. Susan carried a tremendous amount of shame. She felt that her parents didn't love her because she was shy, unattractive, the wrong gender, and generally unacceptable. This overwhelmed Susan, and she lived her life believing that she was a mistake.

HEALTHY GUILT

Authentic, healthy guilt comes from inside. It tells you that you have stepped outside your ethical boundaries. It says, "I have made a mistake or a judgment error. I am responsible for *my* part in that decision." Having feelings of regret or remorse about a decision or an action you've taken is one way some people describe guilt. Other people may say, "I feel bad about that" or "my conscience is bothering me." "I made a mistake" means that your decision was wrong, but that statement does not permanently damage your personal value or worth. All humans make mistakes, and most of the time you deal with the consequences of your mistakes. However, making the mistake does not make you a worthless individual: Your innate value as a person is still intact.

Authentic guilt causes you to freely want to make amends and to come to peace with yourselves and others. Once you respond to your guilt in this way, it does not plague you any longer. You are free to move on. Susan and Mike knew that they had made a mistake and were willing to be responsible for the pregnancy. They both wanted to make it right. They believed they loved each other enough to marry and parent their child. We are certainly not saying that marriage is always the answer. It is important, however, to take ownership of your mistakes and be willing to act responsibly.

UNHEALTHY SHAME

Volumes have been written on the subject of shame, and it is not practical for us to address the issue fully here. Our purpose is to specifically target shame as it relates to Post-Abortion Stress. If you would like to read further about shame, the resources listed in Appendix E are a good place to start.

Shame is a powerful emotion that causes you to believe that you are worthless. The message you hear and respond to is not "I *made* a mistake" but "I *am* a mistake."

Unlike guilt, which is internal and serves a healthy function in your life, shame originates outside you. You are shamed by other people, and this destroys your self-image. There are two major sources of shame.

First, shame is learned through the conditional love messages received from parents, teachers, siblings, and friends. Any message that you get from someone that lets you know their love and care for you is dependent upon your behavior, appearance, or achievement is a conditional love message. Parents withdraw their love as punishment. Emotional support is only given when children meet certain expectations. Friendships are discarded when one person doesn't get what they want. Relationships end when demands for sex or an abortion are not met. These few examples illustrate the way conditional love manifests itself. The underlying belief behind this behavior is that you are not lovable because you don't measure up.

Second, abuse of any kind also creates shame. The abuse can be physical, emotional, sexual, or verbal. A primary message received from the abuser is that the person deserves this abuse. The earlier a person begins to hear these messages, the deeper they sink into her subconscious mind. By the time she reaches adulthood, she is not only reacting to her current circumstances, but also all of her past experiences. Each shame experience builds on the next one. Somehow you believe you have caused your victimization.

Because shame is so powerful, it burrows deep into your soul, the very center of who you are. It continues to generate pain for years. Emotionally, the first reaction to shame is feeling overwhelmed. No matter how you respond to a situation, there is no relief from your feelings of shame. It is like being trapped in a whirlwind with no way out. The more you try to be worthwhile, the more you see your shortcomings. This cycle is called being shame-based.

What adds fuel to the fire of shame in your life? The type of messages you tell yourself is the first way the fire is fed. These are the things you have come to believe about yourself over the years, consciously or unconsciously, as a result of conditional love messages or abuse. Many women say: "I am no good"; "I am stupid"; "I am totally responsible for getting myself pregnant"; "I have to bear the full weight of this pregnancy and decision alone"; "If anyone finds out I will be judged and condemned"; "I have to live with this secret the rest of my life"; "I am not worthy or capable of being a mother"; "I am not worthy to be in a healthy relationship with a man"; "I've had one abortion, why not another?"; "I must look for ways to abuse myself or allow others to abuse me because that's what I deserve." This last statement in particular usually operates on an unconscious level.

The second fuel that adds to your shame base is behavior. Sometimes women who have had an abortion choose, again consciously or subconsciously, certain behaviors and lifestyles that add more shame to their lives. Addictions, abusive relationships, eating disorders, isolation, and secret-keeping keep women stuck in the self-fulfilling prophecy of worthlessness.

How do these messages and behaviors add to your shame base? They add weight to what you already believe: that you are a no-good, worthless person. Shame tells you that you are a failure. The messages haunt you until it seems that they are the only thing you can believe about yourself. Even the smallest mistake can bring thunderous words of shame into your head. One rejection and you give up for months. It's as if each experience adds another brick for you to carry. Life quickly becomes overwhelming.

BREAKING THE CYCLE

But there is hope. We don't in any way mean to imply there is no way out of the shame trap. Though it will take time, shame's power can be broken.

In order to break out of shame or to respond to your guilt in a healthy way, you first need to distinguish between the two. If you recognize guilt about something you have said or done, you will want to make amends in some way. Apologize, seek forgiveness, stop the behavior, pay someone back, or forgive yourself for your mistake. Once you have made amends or restitutions, your feelings of guilt will dissipate.

And how do you recognize shame in your life? The major feelings associated with shame are worthlessness, inadequacy, fear of intimacy, and lack of trust. Shame also overwhelms you with oppressive thoughts and feelings. You may want to run and hide, or you may become extremely defensive.

Everyone feels shame at different times. Everyone has her own very personal and deeply felt shaming experiences. These undoubtedly had some effect on how you responded to your pregnancy and abortion. Susan learned early to feel ashamed of herself, to believe she was worthless. Her desire to act based on her own conscience was impossible because she was overwhelmed by her shame.

What about you? We have found the following questions helpful in understanding your feelings of shame and guilt.

The Traps of Shame and Guilt

1. When have you felt shamed or unworthy?

2. Can you list some of the conditional ways that significant people in your life have cared for you?

3. What happens to you physically and emotionally as you think about those times?

4. How do you want to respond?

5. How do you actually respond?

6. What were the messages you thought you would hear if your pregnancy was "found out"?

7. What were the things you actually did hear?

8. Whose approval do you seem to want the most?

9. Whose disapproval do you fear the most?

10. How do you feel about these people and their conditional love?

11. How significant a part did these feelings play in your decision to get an abortion?

12. How do you feel when you desperately want someone's approval and don't get it?

13. How do you feel about yourself when you are out with friends?

14. How do you feel about yourself when you are with your family?

15. How do you feel when you are out in a crowd of people you don't know very well?

16. Can you distinguish between guilt and shame in your life?

17. How have the feelings of guilt or shame played a part in your reaction to your abortion?

RELEASING THE GRIP

After you distinguish your shame from your guilt, the next step is to release yourself from the grip of shame and replace the lies you have believed.

Shame is powerful, but truth is more powerful. You may not believe there is any way to rectify what you have done or who you are. Everything in your life may seem to confirm that "I always fall short." Though quite unconscious on your part, shame may lie there, bruising you every day.

Truth defeats your shame. Living in truth daily will take some effort and a close evaluation of your thoughts and behavior. If you are shame-based, then most of your words and the words you hear from others are shaming. They may not have been meant that way, but shame-based people—you—hear them that way. Instead of reacting emotionally, you need to clearly sift through what is true and not true in every situation that brings up any feelings of guilt or shame.

It's a lot like beginning an exercise program. You spend the first few weeks with aching muscles. But you keep going back until you work out the soreness. If you stop exercising, the stiff muscles will eventually stop hurting, but you would still be in the same old physical shape.

To change you must learn new ways of thinking and of treating yourself. It will take a few months to see clear changes in your feelings and reactions. When regular exercise becomes a habit, you become a different person physically. In the same way, regularly replacing your shame messages with the truth will make you new emotionally and mentally. Here are some very important truths to help you.

Truths to Break the Cycle of Shame

1. Any decisions, thoughts, or actions I have made as a result of my shame-base were not and are not healthy. They are based on lies about my identity and value.

2. I do not have to continue to let the shame run my life.

3. I must change the beliefs that I hold about myself and others because of being shamed, such as "I am worthless"; "No one can be trusted."

4. My decision to get an abortion has not made me a person with no value.

5. Healing my shame begins with awareness, acknowledgment, and acceptance of the truth.

6. I can have healthy, adult-to-adult relationships that include mutual respect, trust, and love.

7. I need to recognize authentic guilt and respond appropriately.

8. I must acknowledge and face the unhealthy ways that I currently hide my shame or guilt.

Many of our clients use two tools to sort out their thoughts and ideas about shame. The first tool is a self-talk record. Basically, this helps you recognize the things you are telling yourself on a daily basis. Once you have identified the shaming things you continually tell yourself, you can begin to replace these with true statements. Over the next week, keep a record of the things you tell yourself. When you are overwhelmed by any feelings attached to these messages, counter them with the truth.

What I Say	**What Is the Truth**

The second tool in this process is to keep a record of what triggers your shame feelings and how you react. This will help you evaluate and track your progress so you can teach yourself new ways to handle your shame and guilt.

Answer these five questions about each incident where you feel either guilt or shame:

1. What happened?

2. Who was involved?

3. What were my initial feelings?

4. How did I react?

5. How did I feel after my reaction?

Only you can unlock the trapdoor that has held you in a prison where your life has been motivated by your guilt and shame. From personal experience we can assure you that one day you will realize that unlocking this trapdoor is worth any amount of work. We know that seeing yourself as a worthwhile, valuable individual makes *all* the difference in your ability to live life fully.

CHAPTER NINE

Take the Lid Off

Healing Step 5: My post-abortion anger is a pressure cooker that gives me the illusion of power and hides my deeper pain. I will learn to express my angry feelings in a constructive way, so that I don't explode. I will also uncover and deal with the deeper pain that lies beneath my anger.

Your anger about your abortion may come from the deeper feelings about what happened or how you were treated during your pregnancy and abortion. These emotions cause you to feel vulnerable; your anger covers up all other emotions and gives you a feeling of power. Holding on to this anger creates the illusion that this power will keep you from getting hurt again.

Remember Nancy's outbursts of anger? They intensified as her drinking increased. She was caught in the trap of shame from years of you-don't-measure-up messages from her parents. With the additional pain from the abortion, she often found herself stuck in anger and feeling helpless.

Shame left unattended almost always leads to anger. That anger expresses itself as anger at yourself or as rage directed at others. Your anger may even spin around in circles, and ricochet from yourself to other people and back again.

Many people get stuck when it comes to anger. They just don't know what to do with it, whether it is theirs, or someone else's. Everyone knows people who openly, spontaneously, and appropriately express their anger—as well as others who explode in outbursts of rage or act out their anger in very unacceptable ways.

Many parents didn't know how to deal with their anger either, so they were very poor role models. More often than not they modelled pouting, taking pot shots, slamming doors, or pretending nothing was wrong. Other times they expressed anger as rage directed in abusive ways such as screaming, hitting, or destroying property. This behavior had no rhyme or reason and was directed at whoever was there, always out of proportion to the situation.

Sometimes the childhood message about anger was very clear: "Don't let anybody see you angry. Don't yell, scream, or even talk loudly"; "Don't be angry." This don't-talk-about-it-or-show-anger rule is one of the great injustices in society. Because of it, many people don't know what healthy anger is or how to express it.

Examine your experiences with anger as a child. You may still have questions about anger and yet be repeating the patterns you learned because you don't know how else to deal with your anger.

- What were the early messages you received about being angry?
- How did you learn to express it?
- Was being angry the unpardonable sin?
- Were you shushed?
- Was your anger seen as a sign of rebellion and harshly punished?
- Did some family members have the right to express anger while others did not?
- How much of what you learned about anger did you question at the time?

Fears about anger may cause you to try, in lots of unhealthy ways, to keep it in check. Anger may control you; when this happens you may hurt yourself and other people. You may have had the painful experience of being the victim of someone else's out-of-control anger. You may fear that someday you will no longer be able to keep your anger in check and will turn into a monster, out of control and raging like an untamed lion.

PASSIVE AND AGGRESSIVE BEHAVIORS

Our anger functions a lot like a pressure cooker. The pot is filled with painful emotions: loss, rejection, abandonment, shame, hurt, sadness, and fear. In order not to feel these things or become vulnerable to the person who hurt you by expressing your pain, you shove your feelings inside the cooker and close the lid on it. This lid is anger. It covers up the contents of the pot and provides the power to keep everything from spilling out.

As the feelings inside the cooker clamor for release, the pressure inside the pot builds up steam. This steam releases itself so that the pressure cooker doesn't explode. The steam that is released represents the two ways anger can be expressed: through passive-aggressive behavior or aggressive behavior. Whether passive or aggressive ways are used to express anger, the result is the same. The pressure of underlying emotions is relieved for the time being until the pressure builds up again, creating the need to let off more steam.

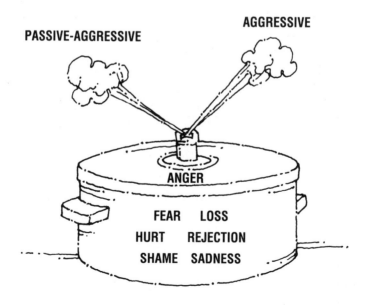

Passive-aggressive anger is covered up or disguised in some way out of one's fear of directly expressing it. Disguised anger comes out in actions like calling names, cursing under your breath, or being perpetually late. Susan used passive-aggressive anger to get back at her folks. Susan and Mike expressed their anger and rebellion by eloping. They were not honest with their folks about their feelings since they did not believe talking with them again would accomplish anything. Susan was also afraid of her father's anger and knew she wouldn't be able to hold her ground in a fight with him. Initially, Susan and Mike didn't realize they were reacting out of anger, but the message they wanted to send was clear: "We'll show them. We'll do something they can't stop or control. We'll be happy, and we'll have another baby." Underneath the lid was all the shame, rejection, hurt, and abandonment they had felt for years, as well as the painful emotions surrounding Susan's abortion.

Aggressive anger explodes, screams, is abusive, rages, or breaks things. This anger yells, "I'll get you and I don't care who knows." It is usually an overreaction and is indiscriminate in its direction. The cycle begins with pushing down painful feelings, then getting angry, and finally exploding. Often the explosion has been triggered by the current situation but is really a response to old emotions. You'll recall that Nancy began exploding angrily at her mom and any guy in her path. She indiscriminately raged at whoever was in the bar when her emotions tried to bubble to the surface. Her anger was out of control and that is what finally led her to get help.

WHAT IS ANGER?

Before moving to anger that is specifically about your abortion, we want to look with you at some of the basic misconceptions people have about anger and also what we believe are the truths about anger.

Anger is a *valid* part of your healing process. It is normal to feel angry in response to your painful abortion feelings.

Misconceptions about Anger

1. Anger is bad.

2 Good people don't get angry.

3. Anger always means you yell, throw things, hurt people, and get it out of your system any way you want.

4. If I get angry, it is always better to pretend that I am not.

5. When another person does not meet my expectations, I should stay angry until they change.

6. When someone does something I don't like or treats me in a way I don't want to be treated, I have a *right* to my anger.

Truth about Anger

1. All humans get angry.

2. Anger is a feeling, one that is not good or bad.

3. My response to the feeling of anger can be either positive or negative.

4. Being angry does *not* always mean yelling or violence.

5. When someone hurts me or fails to meet my needs and expectations, I need to express my feelings and move on.

6. It is *my* choice how I respond to my anger and *my* choice if I remain angry.

7. Sometimes people do things I don't like. All people are different; they do not and will not always measure up to my standards.

8. I do not have the right to harm myself or anyone else because of my anger.

But, like denial, you must not get stuck in your anger. Left to fester, anger becomes bitterness and resentment, causing you to hold grudges, hate people, or seek revenge until it overtakes your good sense. Every decision you make, every action you take, and every word that you say will be infected by your bitterness.

You may be angry about several things in regard to your abortion experience. Record your thoughts in your journal.

- Did you feel no one was there to help you?
- Did your friends and family reject you?
- How did the father of your baby respond when you told him you were pregnant?
- Were your plans and desires overlooked or pushed aside?
- Did you feel manipulated by other people who claimed to have your best interest at heart?
- Were you treated poorly by the clinic staff or the doctor?
- Have you had the support you needed since the abortion to deal with your feelings?

Susan was really mad at herself for getting pregnant. She was angry at her parents for pressuring her into something she didn't want to do. She was angry that the doctor didn't explain what would happen physically or emotionally. Susan felt manipulated and controlled. And she was angry that she did not get to keep a baby she and Mike had created.

Do any of these situations seem familiar to you? With whom are you still angry?

The father of the baby?
____ for not being there physically, emotionally or financially.
____ for pressuring you into an abortion.
____ for making you choose between him and the baby.
____ for not reacting after the abortion as you expected him to.

Yourself?
____ for becoming pregnant.
____ for caving into the pressure even though you
wanted to keep the baby.
____ for not being able to get over your feelings.
____ for choosing an unhealthy relationship.

Family?
____ for pressuring you into an abortion.
____ for not supporting you.

God?
____ for not intervening and fixing the problem.

Others?
____ for withholding the truth about the procedure.
____ for presenting abortion as the best choice.
____ for not giving you better counsel.

Anger is a normal human emotion which happens spontaneously. Yet anger is a scary emotion. If you admit to feeling anger and deal with it, however, you will be one step closer to healing. The problem is not the emotion of anger; it is what you do in response to anger that causes a problem. The goal is not to eliminate anger but to deal with it in an appropriate way. Anger is a very basic emotion and deserves healthy respect and attention.

Now ask yourself these questions and record your answers.

- What are you angry about in relation to your abortion?
- How have you responded to your anger?
- Do you try to hide it? Does it seep out in passive-aggressive ways?
- Do you act out your anger in aggressive ways?
- Do you find yourself angry to the point of rage in situations that don't deserve that much emotion?
- Who is the target of your anger—family, friends, children, your partner, strangers, yourself?
- If you are the target of your anger, how do you express that? By drinking, overeating, drugs, abusive relationships?

EXPRESSING ANGER APPROPRIATELY

It is very important to learn to express your anger in appropriate non-harmful ways. It is even more important to get in touch with the feelings you are keeping in your pressure cooker. These emotions fuel your anger.

Expressing these emotions verbally is important. Writing about your anger in your journal, writing letters, or writing poetry are other ways to express your anger. These things are not necessarily meant to share or send. Sometimes that is appropriate, but it may not be in your best interest or may cause more problems with the person you are angry with. When you are writing about your anger, focus on two basic questions: What are you angry about? What other feelings are you having at the same time? Try to be as specific as possible about your personal feelings and situation.

We have included two sample letters here.

Anger Letter #1 - Susan's letter to her parents:

Dear Mom and Dad:

> *I need to tell you how angry I am with you for forcing me to have an abortion. I know that you thought it was the best thing for me and definitely in your best interest. We never discussed how I felt before the abortion or after. All that happened was you telling me what had to be done. I had no choice and no chance to say what I wanted. I feel like you forced me to have an abortion and then forced me to shut up about it.*

> *Because we still don't have much of a relationship, it's hard to talk to you about my feelings. I have no idea if you ever think about the abortion or the baby–but I have. Every time I see a little blonde girl, I think about what my baby would look like. She would be five years old now. She was my daughter and your granddaughter.*

> *I have been angry at you ever since we left the clinic that day. I felt like you didn't love me or care about my pain. I even had to go alone. You wouldn't let Mike be with me. I still don't understand why you made me do it.*

I feel that you were mad at me for getting pregnant and didn't want anyone to know "your daughter" "got in trouble." Well, I have been "having trouble" ever since that day—more than ever before.

But now I am going to get well and to let you know how I feel is part of my work.

Anger Letter #2 - Patty's letter to Bob:

Dear Bob:

I remember a night not long after we broke up when I saw you with another woman. You were dancing and having a great time. This woman looked like she was in heaven. I wanted to grab her aside and tell her to be careful, that you will treat her like a queen at first, just as you did me—and then you will begin demanding sex.

In fact, from the perspective I have now, you became demanding, controlling, and self-centered pretty early in our relationship. Not long after we started dating exclusively, you controlled every move I made. And I let you. I was stupid to have done that. When I got pregnant you took even more control. Before I knew it you had the money and an appointment for an abortion.

But you didn't have to go through the abortion—I did. And it hurt—physically and emotionally—and inside of me something died. A part of me always dreamed of marrying a loving, kind man, and the birth of our children would be a wonderful experience. I feel like you stole that from me.

I'm also angry because after the abortion you didn't want to hear about my feelings. You even became angry when I was depressed. I thought about the abortion and you every day. And after seeing you that night, I wondered how many other girls you have done this to and if you will treat the next one and the next one the same way.

How many girls have you taken from, disrespected, and then walked away from? I hate you for that. I hope that you realize someday the pain you have caused and feel the anguish that has been part of my life.

Another way to write about your anger is to write statements such as the ones Susan, Monique, and Patty wrote before their letters. They used the following format:

I feel _____ when you _____ because _____ .

Susan wrote:

I feel angry at Mom *because* she didn't let me think for myself or let Mike be with me *and it made me feel* stupid, little, and alone.

Monique wrote:

I feel angry at God *because He* let me get pregnant *when my other friends got off. I feel angry at* myself *because* I did not really want to have sex with him *and I didn't have the courage to say no.*

Patty wrote:

I feel angry at Bob *because* he ignored my questions about whether the abortion was right *and it made me feel* crazy, immature, and lonely.

Poems are still another way of writing about your anger. Here is one that Penny wrote shortly after her abortion.

> Flooding me,
> Waves crashing against my life,
> Emotions embracing me
>   tighter and tighter,
>   crushing me.
> I can't scream out to you;
>   answer me . . .
>   Take my anger.
> Hold me as a child again!
>   Feel my tears of hurt
>   and disappointment.

Free me from this suffocation.
Lift me up and
 give me peace.

The goal is to get to the deepest root of your anger, the underlying feelings of hurt, fear, and rejection. As you write, these emotions will loosen their grip on you. Letting go of anger also includes placing responsibility for actions where it belongs.

This is a painful process. It may seem as if the anger and pain will overwhelm you, but it is far better than allowing the pressure of anger to continue controlling your life.

Here are other helpful and healthy ways of expressing anger:

1. Talk about the anger, as well as the feelings beneath it with a trusted friend.

2. Place an empty chair in front of you and, one at a time, imagine that each person you're angry with is in the chair. Tell each one why you are angry and how it feels.

3. Hit a couch or the bed with a plastic cola bottle or pillow. Go for a run or fast walk. Engage in some physical activity. While you are releasing your pent-up physical energy, say how angry you are and what your life has been like. Cry about the pain.

You may find additional methods that work for you. There is no one right or wrong method, as long as you do not hurt yourself or anyone else.

Anytime anger about your abortion seems to be returning, you may need to repeat the method of expression that worked best for you. This *does not* mean you have not worked out your anger; it just indicates there may be a deeper piece that you need to release.

Finally, the last goal is to learn to recognize issues that make you angry on a daily basis as they arise. You need to change your old patterns of pushing down your painful emotions and recognize trigger events that bring up anger.

Learning to deal with daily trigger events is a healthy result of anger work. Your attitude about anger will be improved and the way you express your anger will be different. You are moving forward . . . out from behind your protective wall. Once the lid is off, the pressure no longer builds to the point of explosion.

You may feel exhausted after this chapter. Rest, take a day or so off, and let your feelings settle. The hard work you have done here will be very beneficial as we move to chapter 10. We certainly encourage you to pursue help with other issues where you still have anger. Some great books are listed in Appendix E to help with further anger work.

CHAPTER TEN

Do Not Surrender to Depression

Healing Step 6: Long-term depression over my abortion robs me of the ability to live a healthy, productive life. Depression consumes all of my energy. I can learn not to surrender to crippling depression.

If you have ever struggled with depression, you probably can identify with some of these lines:

> My bones ache
> My body clothed in despair
> I stare through time's window
> > past shivering bare branch
> > shrouded in hanging fog
> > to dimly lit street lights
>
> so too
>
> The earth heaves
> Covered in thick lifeless air
> Lying in winter sleep
> > the season dying hard . . .
> > silent cold fingers cling
> > with hopeless longing for sun.
> > > Penny

I am bowed down and brought very low;
all day long I go about mourning.

My back is filled with searing pain;
there is no health in my body.

I am feeble and utterly crushed;
I groan in anguish of heart. . . .

My heart pounds, my strength fails me;
even the light has gone from my eyes.

My friends and companions avoid me
      because of my wounds;
my neighbors stay far away. . . .

I am like a deaf man, who cannot hear,
like a mute, who cannot open his mouth.

(Ps. 38:6–13 NIV)

Depression is a natural response to pain in a person's life. Depression is pressure turned inward, and often the pain becomes deeper when no one understands. It is difficult for those who have not experienced depression to understand it.

Depression has three levels. The first type of depression is situational and occurs to most people at one time or another during their lifetime. Situational depression is a reaction to an event in life, such as a death, a divorce, or the breakup of a relationship. When a person acknowledges her depression and works through her feelings, this level of depression resolves itself in a short period of time and normally does not reoccur.

The second level of depression occurs when a person gets stuck and cannot resolve her depression. She may experience a depression for years, which fluctuates in intensity depending on circumstances. This may even become the way someone has learned to cope with adversity. Typically, this depression reoccurs during certain times of the year or is prevalent around anniversary dates. The root of the problem here is usually the feelings and thoughts that preceded it. Not being able to deal with the abortion leads to depression.

The third type of depression is clinical depression. This type of depression affects a person physiologically, specifically the serotonin and hormone levels. This type of depression usually runs in families and medication can be useful in its treatment. Antidepressants will help the person reach an emotional level in which counseling can be beneficial.

WHAT IS DEPRESSION?

The poem and psalm at the beginning of this chapter are excellent descriptions of depression. We hear women describe depression as a black hole, a deep dark place where they feel oppressed, immobile, and constantly exhausted. These verbal expressions are from depressed women: "I don't want to get up"; "I can't function on any level"; "I don't care about anything."

Some people define depression as the sad feeling we have when we deal with loss. Others say it is anger turned inward. Still others define depression as a feeling of helplessness, of being trapped and without hope. Our experience says that two things are certainly true: Depression is a thief that steals energy and hope, and depression after an abortion does not have to last forever.

As depression depletes energy, you lose desire and the ability to live a productive, healthy life. You may sometimes lose sight of your goals because you feel blocked, chained, and unable to move. In *The Wounded Heart*, Dan Allender stated that the symptoms of depression "include a despondent view of oneself, the world and the future. They (depressed people) have little hope for change and feel as if the weight of the world is upon them."[1]

But this feeling does not have to be a permanent reality in your life. That fact is very important to remember when you are depressed because depression is the stage of grief that robs you of a view into the future. Anyone who has lost a significant person feels depressed because she cannot imagine how her life can go on without her loved one. The weight feels unbearable and the darkness blinds us to hope.

When you surrender to your depression, it becomes your only friend. Along with your energy, depression saps your strength, your will, and your motivation, until it is easier to surrender than to fight. Then you aren't depressed because of loss—you are depressed because this has become a familiar way to deal with your feelings. Because of the overpowering and oppressive nature of depression, some people believe that it is somehow their lot in life. Not true—you can move through, not surrendering to it. Our goal is to help you identify the severity of depression you are experiencing and then help you to walk away from it instead of sinking down in surrender.

Following is a list of the basic symptoms of depression. Later in this chapter is a Post-Abortion Depression Inventory to assess your level of post-abortion depression.

Basic Depression Symptoms

1. Your sleep pattern is disrupted: You are not able to fall asleep easily; you awaken in the night and are not able to get a good night's sleep; you are sleeping much more than is normal for you; you are sleeping during the day or you are not sleeping at all.

2. All activity seems to happen in slow motion.

3. You have no interest in life. You constantly feel bored or numb. You have no interest or involvement in anything.

4. Your self-esteem has hit rock-bottom. You don't think that you are "worth the effort." You are "down on yourself." You think that nothing you think or feel matters anyway.

5. You have a lack of concentration. You are unable to focus on anything for very long. You are easily distracted. You find yourself lost in thought or daydreaming most of the time.

6. You are constantly dwelling on your loss. You have become preoccupied with the feelings and events surrounding your loss.

7. There is a change in your eating habits. You may be eating much more than normal, or you may not be eating at all.

8. You may be struggling with drug and/or alcohol abuse.

9. You may have become totally withdrawn. Though similar to losing interest in life, your behavior is more severe. You have cut off all contact with the outside world. You stay at home and alone much of the time.

10. Your lack of memory is pretty severe. Sometimes you can't remember coming home, whether or not you've eaten, or appointments you've made.

ABORTION-RELATED DEPRESSION

At least part of your depression is a symptom of the ungrieved loss resulting from your abortion. Many women believe that the abortion was their choice, and thus they do not deserve to grieve for their child, that it is not a legitimate loss. If you do feel a sense of loss, you tell yourselves it's wrong to feel that now, so you stuff it inside. This secret pain and sense of loss make depression very complicated and difficult for post-abortion women. Women may experience depression soon after their abortions, or it may come much later.

One morning, three weeks after her abortion, Alice couldn't get out of bed. She felt as if her legs and arms wouldn't move. Her head ached and her stomach was in knots. It was Saturday and she'd had a difficult week at work, so she thought she just needed a day off to rest. Sunday she still felt the same. She stayed in bed most of the day, finally moving to the couch for the afternoon. Monday she felt no better, but she dragged herself off to work anyway. Dressing seemed to take forever. Friends in the office noticed something was wrong, and one look in the mirror proved they were right! She did look pale and drawn. What was happening to her? In the days to come Alice felt a deepening sense of gloom.

One day at lunch Alice saw a little girl and her mom having lunch. All of a sudden Alice started to cry and couldn't stop. She headed home and took some days off work. Alice was normally the strong independent one in the family, so when Alice called her sister in another state, they both knew something was wrong. The phone call caused her sister to book a flight for a long overdue visit with Alice.

Alice and her sister talked for hours. Alice was so relieved to talk to someone she trusted that she got the courage to ask her sister the question that had been on her mind for days now. Could this have anything to do with her abortion? Since her sister had experienced two miscarriages in years past, she knew the heartache and agreed that Alice's feelings sounded very similar. Maybe it was about Alice's abortion.

It took a while before Alice found a therapist who understood what she was experiencing. The first therapist she saw confirmed that she definitely was depressed but didn't believe it could be related to the abortion. It took a couple more tries before she found someone to help her with the abortion losses.

Alice describes that time in her life as being in a survival mode. She could only manage the most basic tasks of life—sleeping, eating, barely working—and even then she felt as if she was only muddling through. No one told her to expect depression, and when it happened she wasn't prepared to handle her emotional black hole. Since she was severely depressed, her doctor recommended a mild medication for awhile. Counseling as well as the strong love, support, and comfort from her sister were all necessary ingredients for Alice's healing.

SYMPTOMS OF POST-ABORTION DEPRESSION

Most women who have an abortion have some depression. It may be milder than Alice's—or much more severe. You may simply walk around feeling numb or disinterested in life for a while. Or your life may be completely beyond your ability to manage. As with every stage of grief, there are degrees in the intensity of your pain. The important thing is to get the help you need in a time frame that's comfortable for you. If, however, you are experiencing clinical depression, you need help immediately.

Let's look at a depression inventory specifically related to abortion. Use the following keys in answering your inventory:

Y–*yes, most of the time*. S–*sometimes*. N–*not often or never*.

Post-Abortion Depression Inventory

____ 1. Immediately after the abortion I felt exhausted.
____ 2. I tend to be more edgy than usual.
____ 3. I am preoccupied with the image of the baby.
____ 4. I feel the abortion experience has aged me.
____ 5. I yearn for the baby.
____ 6. I sometimes feel guilty when I do something that might be enjoyable.
____ 7. I feel guilty because I am still living and my baby is not.
____ 8. I find no comfort in believing my baby is in heaven.

_____ 9. I feel as if something inside me has died.

_____10. My arms and legs feel very heavy.

_____11. I often feel confused.

_____12. I feel lost and helpless.

_____13. I have had frequent headaches since the abortion.

_____14. I cry easily.

_____15. I have taken tranquilizers a lot since the abortion.

_____16. My mouth and throat feel dry a lot of the time.

_____17. I feel restless.

_____18. Concentrating on things is hard for me.

_____19. I feel tense in my neck and shoulders.

_____20. I have the urge to crawl up into a ball.

_____21. Sometimes I just want to scream and scream.

_____22. I don't have the energy to exercise.

_____23. I rarely feel enthusiastic about anything.

_____24. Life has lost its meaning for me.

_____25. I have feelings of apathy.

_____26. I feel as if I just watch myself go through the motions of daily living.

_____27. I am losing a lot of weight.

_____28. I have gained a lot of weight.

_____29. I have lost my appetite.

_____30. I am not interested in sexual activities.

_____31. I wish I were dead.

_____32. I have a special need for someone to talk to.

_____33. It often feels as if I have a lump in my throat.

_____34. I have lost my self-confidence.

_____35. I drink more alcohol now than before the abortion.

_____36. I stay awake most of the night.

_____37. I lose sleep due to worry.

_____38. I often wake in the middle of the night and cannot get back to sleep.

_____39. Things seem blackest when I am awake in the middle of the night.

_____40. I can sleep during the day but not at night.

_____41. I often think about how short life is.

_____42. Small things seem overwhelming.

_____43. My religious faith is a source of strength and comfort.

_____44. I have a special need to be near others.

_____45. I want to be alone a great deal.

_____46. I have isolated myself from most people.
_____47. I hesitate to attend social gatherings.

Go back through the inventory and count the number of yes answers. If you marked twenty-five or more statements yes, you are very depressed and need to find a counselor to help you. Eleven to twenty-four yes answers means you are mildly depressed; however, do not ignore your feelings. Start to work through your grief so your depression doesn't get worse. Ten or less yes answers means that you are experiencing only a small amount of depression. This is not something to worry about unless it gets worse, but do watch for any increase in symptoms.

This inventory is not meant to make you feel worse about yourself. Its purpose is to help you identify the level of your depression so that you can move through it.

Sometimes it is helpful to know whether or not your depression has a pattern. We often find that women struggle with depression more around anniversary dates—the day the child would have been born, and the day of the abortion—as well as around holidays and season changes. One of the most useful ways to look at how your depression cycles is to keep a daily log. Include what symptoms you have, how severe they are, and how long they last. Do your symptoms occur at certain times of the year? Are your symptoms chronic or periodic? Of course, the mere writing about your feelings is therapeutic. Returning to your journal is also a good way to see the progress you've made.

Post-abortion women often stay in depression so long due to the repeated shame and guilt messages they cling to, such as: "I am terrible"; "I can't even be a good mom to the children I have"; "I am ruining my life because of my depression"; "I should be able to get over this." Nightmares, fear, lack of a support system, and isolation also contribute to prolonged depression.

MOVING OUT OF DEPRESSION

Sharing your sorrow, your thoughts, and your feelings is the most effective way to keep from surrendering to your depression. You can do this by talking with someone or by writing in your journal.

As you write, the oppression that has pushed you down begins to lose its grip. As your depression is released, you can open your hands to receive new emotions to replace the depression. You were so filled with negative emotions that nothing else could get in. Now there is room. C. S. Lewis described the process in this way: "It was as if the lifting of sorrow removed a great barrier."[2]

Once again we encourage you to write about these feelings until you can write no more. Write and rewrite. It's like crawling up and out of the hole you are in. You will find the energy that has been drained by your depression and hopelessness slowly returns.

One day soon you will find that your depression is less than the day before. As time goes by it will continue to lift. You will notice you are spending less and less time struggling with depression.

You can overcome the pain of an abortion. As you come out of depression it is like seeing sunshine after many days of cold weather, after days with only dark and rainy skies. There is a whole new world out there with blue skies, light, and hope.

There's a Larry Gatlin song with lines that you may be familiar with, "There's a light at the end of the darkness and a healing balm for pain and misery. It's as near as your *heart* though sometimes it seems fleeting—I was down when it finally *shined* on me." *

Penny wrote the following poem describing depression. We think it captures the moods a woman feels as she struggles to be free from its stranglehold on her life.

How Much More

Where are

      the years, words, love . . .
chiseled away through time
smashed against rocky cliffs
suffocated beneath breathless sighs

      the hopes and dreams . . .
abandoned for lack of faith
beaten to death by fear
ripped away in silent screams

      the flesh of my flesh . . .
broken pieces
shattered again and again
cutting tender edges of care

      the hearts of two . . .
aching heavy, and naked,
filled with shapeless illusion
weeping tears of loneliness

      the empty arms . . .

How much more
How much more
How
      Much
            More

                  Penny

CHAPTER ELEVEN

Find Freedom in Forgiveness

Healing Step 7: I will learn how to forgive myself and others, so that I can break the chains of bondage to my past. Offering and receiving forgiveness frees me to walk into a new life.

The way of wisdom is living.
The path of peace is forgiving.
Michael Card[1]

Any definition of forgiveness begins with certain foundational assumptions about who individuals are in relation to God. Understanding those principles is the foundation for finding freedom in forgiveness.

The first one is basic: Human beings are created in the image of a relational God. This assumption implies that people are made for relationship: with themselves, with others, and with God the Creator. To be in relationship means to love others and be loved in return. There is, therefore, value and purpose in these relationships: mothers with their children, husbands and wives, and teachers with students all find purpose in their relationships.

Our ability to relate enables us to express our innate value and fulfill our unique purpose. But it is in our relationships that we receive our wounds *and* our healing. Before you can work through forgiveness topics, you need to take some time to examine your relationships.

- What relationships come to mind when you think about being wounded?
- What relationships come to mind when you think about being healed in some way?
- How do you think your relationships fulfill you?
- Are some of your relationships more fulfilling than others?

The second assumption is that there is a distinct difference between human beings and God. God embodies some characteristics humans do not possess, most notably His completeness, His ability to love perfectly and unconditionally, and His personal intimacy with each individual. He doesn't break promises or hold grudges; He is faithful, and He has each person's best interest at heart. Humans, on the other hand, make all kinds of mistakes; they break promises to others and to themselves, carry grudges, and sometimes are abusive even to themselves. They are not capable of living lives in perfect harmony with other people, although they can strive toward that harmony.

People carry deep within them a desire to become whole and complete, because that is the way God intended them to be. Now consider your own assumptions about being complete:

- Can you recall any of the things you have done in an attempt to be "complete," like striving to be a perfect mom, to get all A's, to climb to the top of the corporate ladder, or to get married?
- What are some of the things that you have been told or always thought would fill up your heart?

Assumption number three is the belief in the existence of good and evil. God is good, healthy, and life-giving; He brings peace and joy. The sad truth is that the world is not good: evil resides here. The pressure of the "dark side," or evil, causes everyone to make mistakes, to fall short of the mark of completeness. The effects of evil are all around us: poverty, starvation, violent crimes, war, racial hatred, child abuse, and violence within the home. And throughout history, stories and movies speak of this ancient battle between good and evil; the Bible, most fairy tales, Shakespeare's plays, classic novels, and even modern movies such as *Star Wars* and *Batman* are but a few of the many that grapple with this dilemma.

The final assumption is that the Creator gives forgiveness as a way to heal the wounds suffered and to repair broken relationships. If it were not possible to forgive, whole lives would be lived inside the walls of perpetual mistrust and anger. It is impossible to sustain any relationship living like this, for a significant part of relational healing comes through forgiveness. The gift of forgiveness makes it possible to move beyond personal mistakes and the mistakes of others.

Alcoholics Anonymous has helped millions of people who struggle with addictions through support groups and the Twelve-Step Program. An integral part of the Alcoholics Anonymous philosophy is forgiveness and reconciliation. This is embodied in steps 4 through 10 of the Twelve-Step program:

[We]

4. Made a searching and fearless moral inventory of ourselves.

5. Admitted to God, to ourselves, and to another human being the exact nature of our wrongs.

6. Were entirely ready to have God remove all these defects of character.

7. Humbly asked Him to remove our shortcomings.

8. Made a list of all persons we have harmed, and became willing to make amends to them all.

9. Made direct amends to such people wherever possible, except when to do so would injure them or others.

10. Continue to take personal inventory and when we are wrong, promptly admit it. [2]*

What about you?

- Is forgiveness a part of your life?
- Have you ever received genuine forgiveness?
- What did that feel like?
- Have you ever extended forgiveness to someone else?
- What was that like?
- When was the last time you gave yourself a break?
- How did that feel?

WHY FORGIVE?

People are faulty and they live in a world with other faulty people. Their lives are crowded with unmet expectations, broken relationships, abandonment, and choices that hurt themselves or someone else—and all of these things cripple lives in some way. Only forgiveness can bring healing.

First, *forgiveness restores hearts* and even relationships. Lewis B. Smedes, author of the book *Forgive and Forget: Healing the Hurts We Don't Deserve*, writes: "forgiving is the only way we have to a better fairness in our unfair world. It is love's unexpected revolution against unfair pain and it alone offers strong hope for healing the hurts we so unfairly feel."[3]

Forgiveness opens the door to possibilities and life, instead of forcing you to live in the darkness of bitterness and death. Forgiveness is a far better risk than living the way you have, carrying your abortion pain alone. When you hold

---

* See Appendix A for a listing of the Twelve Steps in their entirety.

on to your abortion and don't forgive yourself and others, you are held captive to the past. It is virtually impossible to do anything without the chains of "what was" holding you back and causing you to second guess all decisions.

Second, *forgiveness releases emotions.* Forgiveness makes you stronger. In forgiving, you confront and deal with the reality of your life; energy is freed from attending to the steady buildup of the anger pressure cooker. You no longer spend time grappling with the "Why me?"; "How could they?"; and "What happened?" questions. And the relentless search for justification and restitution can end.

Finally, *forgiveness renews life.* You no longer have to be a victim. You are free to re-evaluate your relationships and to set healthy boundaries. You can then follow the path of forgiveness to peace—with yourself and others.

WHAT IS FORGIVENESS?

Forgiveness is a release from holding yourself or someone else guilty for your actions. The choice you made and the choices of others concerning your abortion have marked your life in a profound way. The act of forgiveness gives a "new marking," a turning of the path away from the past toward renewed relationship with yourself, others, and God.

Most importantly, forgiveness is the doorway through which we can walk away from past bondage, begin to live fully in the present, and look forward to the future. You can see damaging actions that have affected your life in a new way. The power of forgiveness moves you away from your past pain and the endless chain of reactions. It creates a new situation to which you then can respond without being overwhelmed by negative emotions that keep wounds festering.

Forgiveness acknowledges pain and comes to understand better the events that led up to the abortion. Forgiveness is a matter of the heart—to see and to feel the pain. If forgiveness is only an intellectual exercise, it does not work. Many times we forgive someone in an offhand way. It is something we do because it smooths things over; because we don't care for conflict; because we believe we have to; or because someone insists. If this is the case, the power of forgiveness is empty because we have not taken a true accounting of the situation. And in order for forgiveness to effect change in your life, it must come with an emotional conviction.

The last two characteristics of forgiveness are that it be freely given and given often. No one can force your heart to forgive. You must *choose* to enter into the process of forgiving, but it is a choice you make for your well-being. Forgive yourself and others for every offense and forgive often. This is the only way to live in a world with grace and growth.

BLOCKS TO FORGIVENESS

Many things stand in your way when you need to forgive. Because these blocks are overwhelming, you may shy away from forgiveness.

First, forgiving is a hard thing to do. Holding on to anger and fear is the natural response to injury; it is natural not to extend forgiveness. Anger is an emotion that makes a person feel powerful; without it she may feel disarmed. One of our clients put it this way: "My anger felt like this powerful weapon I could use whenever I needed it. The idea of forgiving felt like I would become defenseless. I thought, 'Why would I want to do something that stupid?' Once I began to see that the only person who was getting wounded was myself, I decided I would just stop fighting the war. That's what forgiving did for me. I no longer needed the weapon because I was no longer part of the battle."

Because feeling the pain is a prerequisite to forgiveness, you sometimes think you can't face it. Another client said: "It helps me want to forgive when I remember that I felt like I was rotting away inside physically and emotionally by not letting go of the pain."

The second block to forgiving is that you often try to let yourself and others off the hook by justifying behavior. You need to understand that forgiveness is not about excusing behavior that hurts people. You forgive people for things you blame them for; you forgive people for the bad things they have done. In order to be able to forgive someone, you need to honestly and clearly evaluate what happened. You don't forgive unless you can first place responsibility where it belongs. Be specific about what the wrong action was and the degree of pain that resulted.

The third block to forgiving can best be explained like this: "I can't forgive myself because I can never forget what happened." This response is not only heard in our counseling but is a common reaction to the idea that forgiving means forgetting. The truth is that forgiveness is not about forgetting what happened: You need to remember what has happened in your life in order to make changes. The past shapes who you are and the decisions you make. Forgetting may lead you back into letting others treat you badly. You need to remember so that you don't tolerate injustice or bad behavior again. We call this "redemptive remembering," a way to integrate painful memories. In this kind of remembering you don't dwell on the past but instead focus on the fact that you were released from your pain.

The other side to this issue is this: Because we cannot forget we sometimes feel as if forgiveness hasn't happened. Most of us falsely believe that if we have truly forgiven or been forgiven we shouldn't feel any more pain. However, there is something profoundly sad about things that can't be changed: You cannot have this baby back; many relationships cannot be fixed.

The fourth block to forgiveness is this: Why do I have to forgive him if he's not sorry? Women ask this question about their boyfriends, their doctors, and their parents. They feel as if they are being cheated if they forgive someone who isn't sorry. The trouble with this misconception is that some people aren't sorry, we can't make them sorry, and holding on only hurts us.

Monique had this to say about Peter: "It was like keeping my boyfriend in a cage in my heart—every once in a while I would take him out and beat up on him. I realized that he didn't even know. I wasn't hurting him; I was just reliving my pain over and over again. You know, it really did hurt enough the first time." Monique finally realized that Peter was never going to say, "I'm sorry for hurting you." If she waited for an apology she would never be free.

The fifth block to making forgiveness a tool in healing is thinking you need to earn forgiveness. Many of our clients discover that they have been doing things for years in order to earn forgiveness for themselves. Trying to earn forgiveness will only leave you empty. The question then becomes "How many times is enough?" or "Will there ever be enough?" We believe that forgiveness is a gift of grace to receive. It cannot and must not be contingent on your behavior.

The last block is the concept of forgiving God. Monique struggled with this; she felt angry at and hurt by God. She began each day for years telling God she was sorry about her abortion but she never felt better. She couldn't reconcile her thoughts that God could have prevented the pregnancy and abortion or at least changed Peter's mind or her circumstances. She struggled with her own feelings of responsibility for her choices. To top it all off, she thought that she might be wrong in being angry at God. As Monique shared these things in counseling and was reassured that her struggles were a normal response to her pain, she realized that her feelings were okay. This freedom gave her the willingness to talk to God honestly and let go of her anger.

HOW TO FORGIVE

Forgiveness happens on different levels: forgiving yourself, forgiving other people, and asking forgiveness from another. Although there are some differences, the basic process of forgiving is the same. It's important to realize who you need to forgive and what you need to forgive them for. You will also need to think about those you need to ask for forgiveness.

The place most of our clients get stuck in the forgiving process is when they confront the need to forgive themselves. Here are some of the struggles they face:

I don't think badly about someone else who got an abortion. I just can't seem to give myself any room for mistakes.

I can't get over the fact that I let myself down. I caved in to the pressure. I should have been stronger.

I really think that if I was to forgive myself, I would have to stop hurting. If I didn't feel my pain I would somehow be saying that the baby wasn't important.

I feel so ashamed I can't forgive myself. Surely this is the worst thing anyone has ever done.

Sometimes it is a little difficult to discover exactly what you need to forgive yourself for. Consider these questions and spend time responding in your journal.

- Did you let yourself down?
- Did you go against your gut feelings?
- Do you blame yourself for everything?
- Do you blame someone else for everything?
- Have you done or said things in response to your abortion that you now regret?

Next, as you make a decision to forgive others, you may struggle with confusion about how you feel and what your expectations are. You may still feel angry at them or about the situation. Do you want the other person to be sorrier, hurt more, or take back their words and actions? Maybe you want to get even. Even after you forgive, you may continue to be angry. In other words, you make a decision to forgive even if you don't feel like it. The feelings of anger and pain sometimes take a while to subside. Remember, forgiveness is an action you take, not necessarily a feeling you have.

Finally, if there are hurtful things that you have done or said to another person, you may want to ask forgiveness from them. Most of our clients find they want to ask forgiveness from their babies. Those clients who have a relationship with God also seek forgiveness from Him. Examine your own feelings. The answers to these questions will point you in the direction of how and when to ask forgiveness from someone else.

- Do you feel that your actions or responses to your abortion experience have caused a break in your relationship with anyone?
- What are your feelings about wanting to repair that damage?

In preparing to forgive someone or in asking for forgiveness, you need to decide if you will deal personally with the people involved. We hold to the same belief as expressed by Alcoholics Anonymous in step 9: Only talk with people personally if doing so will not injure them, others, or yourself. We encourage our clients to ask themselves what their motives are in a personal approach and what can be gained by talking with the person. Our rule of thumb is to follow your heart. Sometimes well-thought-out letters written to express your emotions, but never sent, work well. We also feel that forgiveness is largely an issue between you and God. He certainly can let you know what you need to do in cases where it is not safe to go directly to the people who were involved.

We encourage you to enter into the act of forgiveness with your whole heart and with a solid understanding of what forgiveness is about. If you need more information we suggest reading Lewis B. Smedes's *Forgive and Forget* or looking at *The Twelve-Step Program* from Alcoholics Anonymous.

When you are ready to begin the process of forgiving, make a list of the people you feel you need to forgive. This list will probably be very similar to the list of people you were angry with that you made in Chapter 9. The list may include the father of the baby, your parents, your doctor, friends, church or support community, yourself, or God.

After you have made your list, make another list of specific things you are willing to forgive each person for. Looking over your journal or any letters you have written may help you get in touch with some of these things.

The next step is deciding to forgive. You may need to push yourself here a little, because most people never *feel* like forgiving. You may not be ready at this point to forgive certain things, and that's okay. Forgiving and healing is a process and it happens at a different rate for everyone. Start where you can and as long as you continue to be honest and desire healing, the rest will come. Forgiveness can come a little at a time.

Once you have set your will to forgive, take your list and verbally forgive each person and each offense. It may go something like this:

Mom, I forgive you for insisting I get an abortion.

Peter, I forgive you for leaving me alone to work this out.

Doctor, I forgive you for not telling me about fetal development.

I forgive *myself* for caving in to my fear and confusion.

After you have verbally forgiven each person, we strongly suggest that you destroy your list. This will ensure your privacy as well as serve as a symbolic gesture about your decision to forgive and release yourself from the past.

You may be asking this question next: "How do I know I have experienced forgiveness?" Since this occurs in a different way for each person, we asked some of our clients to share with you about their experiences:

Denise:

I told a friend about my abortion. At that point I began to deal with some of my anger, bitterness, and resentment toward the aborted baby's father. That was a major area where God worked forgiveness in my heart. It was gradual and I can't say that I just did it one day, but the resentment faded over maybe a period of months or a year or so to the point that I am now able to wish the best for him.

However, I do think that forgiveness—true forgiveness from the heart—is a work of God in us. At that point, I was willing, and God worked it in me.

Forgiveness is certainly a central issue in healing after an abortion. In my experience there were several areas or stages.

Carol:

Forgiveness is something that was a long time coming to me, not because God did not want it for me, but because I could not accept it for so long.

My first abortion was when I was sixteen and desperate. My second was when I was eighteen, married, and pressured into it by my husband. Getting pregnant is not something you do by yourself, yet I took on all the blame and guilt. Feeling unworthy was my normal mode.

I have had counseling and have deepened my relationship with God. I have accepted forgiveness in my heart in full.

There are moments when I remember something about my abortions that feels as sharp as a razor. Once when I was feeling sad about my abortions, my son held my face and said, "What's the matter, Mama?" I looked into his big brown eyes and I saw God's grace infinitum. I see so much of God's love through my son. God has carried me to a point in my life where I see His hand has really been carrying me all of my life. If He cherished me that much, then I cannot be so bad.

Vicki:

My experiences with forgiveness came in two distinct ways. One was a "light bulb" experience. After a long struggle to replace my loss through foster parenting, it became clear to me that I was trying to work out my forgiveness. That had happened fourteen years earlier when I first knew how sorry I was that I let my mother push me into getting an abortion. The light came on for me and I knew that I wasn't living as if I was forgiven. There was no act of restitution that could change what happened.

The second way, which is much harder, is the slow process of forgiving someone else. I knew that I had forgiven my mother when my angry, hateful thoughts weren't there any longer. I began to recognize that I had started to see her as a person who needed compassion. Sometimes it is still a daily decision to be forgiving in that relationship.

Christine:

The feeling of forgiveness was like a tight vise, or binding cord, had been released off my heart and all through my body. Then warmth flooded through me, followed by the most soft, gentle, almost golden-like peace that I had ever felt before. Something so pure, and kind, a caressing feeling of love filled my heart. For once in my life I felt whole, no longer in pieces or trying to justify who I was. The tears just flowed and flowed out of me.

The feeling of forgiveness gave me permission and courage to tell the shame to leave me for good. Shame was the buckle that kept the binding cord of fear around my heart and God's forgiveness was the key that unlocked it and set me free. No longer would I be bound up in shame—my abortion, the memories, and pain were exposed to the light and I could finally face it all. My counselors became my witnesses along the journey to wholeness.

As you take your steps toward making forgiveness a part of your healing, we hope that you, too, find *your heart has been restored, your emotions released, and your life renewed.*

CHAPTER TWELVE

Become Reconciled

Healing Step 8: I have grieved my abortion losses and taken back my life. I can now focus my attention on the present by reclaiming the inner beauty God has given me through unconditional self-acceptance and love.

Becoming reconciled is about "closure," integration, and embracing life in its fullest sense. Our deepest hope is that this chapter will enable you to do these things.

In recent years terrorists have captured and held Americans in several hostage situations. The media in Tennessee gave particular attention to one hostage, his situation, and to the effort to secure his release.

He experienced five long years as a victim of terrorists who tortured their hostages. He did not see the light of day for at least three years. At times he was able to communicate with other hostages, but during other long periods no communication was allowed.

After several years the hostages were released one by one and this man was the last. His mind went from wondering if he would ever get out to how he would find the world when he was released. Would he know how to function "outside the darkness" after being confined for so long? By necessity, he had learned how to function within the confines set by terrorists. His desire to live was strong, and he hoped he would learn to function as a free man once again.

Some of his time was spent imagining the changes that were occurring in the world and in his own family. What would they be like? Did they still know and love him? Would he be able to relate to people who hadn't had this experience?

Finally the day came and he was released. His wife and daughter were the first to see him. The reunion was bittersweet: to be with one another brought joy inexpressible, but the realization of the years lost was a saddening shock.

Integrating his experiences as a tortured hostage into his newfound freedom was the task now before him. He was wise enough to seek professional help both physically and emotionally. He learned how to regain his physical health with proper food and exercise. He worked through his feelings, identified and grieved his losses as he talked about being in prison and his release. There were so many things he needed to share: terrors, doubts, and fears that he had suffered and the nightmares that haunted him now. The therapist also helped him and his family learn how to communicate with one another again. After years of nothing but isolation and abuse, he struggled to handle a loving relationship again.

Slowly his lifestyle, thoughts, and feelings readjusted. He had been in darkness for a long, long time; now there was light. He would tell you today that reunion and adjusting were slow and tough but worth *every* minute. He would also say that learning to walk in freedom was an invaluable gift and that having the opportunity to love and be loved is the greatest treasure of a lifetime. From darkness into light—from death to new life—saying good-bye and hello in the same moment—that is the next step in this grieving process.

We have told you this story because we believe it parallels the kind of experience that many post-abortion women struggle with. Their pain and sorrow have held them captive for many years. They have been isolated with anger, shame, and fear constantly beating down their soul. Coming to grips with the reality of their abortion losses and grieving those losses brings them to the same place of reconciliation that this former hostage came to—saying good-bye and saying hello—to light and a new life.

RECONCILING WITH YOUR CHILD

The first part of bringing closure to your abortion experience is reconciling with your child. This step begins with a name and an identity. Some of you have carried in your heart the name you would have given this baby. In your mind and heart this child has an individual, unique identity. We talked earlier about the importance of a name. If you have not given your child a name, think about doing so now. Most of our clients find that being able to say their baby's name instead of referring to "the baby" or "my abortion" provides them with a missing piece. Monique said, "Being able to talk about James and using his name finally gave me the feeling that my family was complete." Renee commented after sharing what she had named her child: "As soon as I named her, that emptiness in my heart began to fill up."

If your child had lived, he or she would have had a unique personality, appearance, and talent. You can never know exactly what these things would be. However, many women find it comforting to imagine what their child's future would have been. The only memories you may have of your pregnancy and abortion experience are filled with negative feelings and those which cause you pain. Giving your child a name and imagining the kind of person they would be will help you add to these memories, making it easier for you to finish your grieving.

Allow some memories to be made about your child.

- In your imagination what would your child have been like?

- What physical characteristics do you suppose your baby would have? Brown eyes? Curly hair? Your nose?
- Would she love to read, or be musical? Would he hate math and have a great sense of humor?

At some point every woman who is grieving her aborted child has a desire to communicate with that child. She may wonder, "Where is my baby now?" "Does he understand what happened and why I made this decision?" "What kind of a mother does she think I am?" "If I see her in heaven, will she know I'm her mother?"

The second step in reconciling with your baby is saying good-bye. When someone dear to us suddenly dies, one of the biggest regrets is not getting to have that last talk, not saying the things we always meant to. In essence, not saying good-bye leaves us with an open wound.

We do not have all the answers, and we certainly do not advocate "calling people from the dead." However, our experience is that women need to reconcile with their babies in their own hearts. In group and individual therapy, we ask women to picture their baby, imagine holding him or her in their arms and saying the things they've always wanted to say; and then, when they are ready, imagine saying good-bye and symbolically giving the baby back to God. Some women find this is too difficult so they choose instead to write a letter or poem to their baby. These things are a labor of love written with tenderness and truth. You will find some of these expressions at the end of the chapter.

We believe that all aborted babies are with God. He cherishes every life. You can trust Him to take care of your child now. As Patty reconciled with her baby daughter, Patty had a dream that she could see several little children playing in a yard. Two of them came over to the picket fence and peered over the top. Patty recognized them immediately— one was her aborted daughter and the other little girl was her sister's aborted baby. Patty's little girl called out, "Mommy, it's wonderful here. I love you." Patty woke up, knowing in her heart that her daughter was part of a wonderful family in heaven. She says it's good to know that her child has only known perfect love.

When someone close to you dies, you may think of them often and desire to be with them again. Positive memories of times spent together help you hold on to the reality of that person's impact on your life and kindles the hope of a reunion. Unfortunately, when you have lost your child through abortion, these memories are not available, which makes the grief process a little more difficult. Wishing you had a picture of your child or a memento of theirs or that you could know what your baby's features would have been like is not strange, but rather is part of the grief process.

The last step in reconciling with your baby is putting in place some kind of memorial. Memorials give a reminder of the person you loved and lost. All cultures have elaborate customs to remember their dead; funerals, wakes, and memorial services provide a way to honor the passing of a human life. They also give a way for us to openly acknowledge the reality of our grief to the world.

Most often a memorial is visible, but for some women it is a place in their heart. When a relative or friend dies, a tombstone of some sort is commonly erected. In chapter 1, we examined the importance of the Vietnam Memorial in Washington, D.C., for veterans, their family and friends, as well as the nation. We encourage you to find an appropriate memorial so you have something that holds the memory of your child.

Renee bought a wreath that is actually two wreaths in one, a smaller one tucked inside the larger one. It contains a nest with two small birds inside. This now hangs in her home as a special reminder of her aborted babies, the circle of life, and her hope for the future.

It took Nancy several years after her initial grief work to find a memorial for her daughter, Victoria. Then on a summer camping trip in the Black Canyon in western

Colorado, Nancy discovered the perfect place to say her final good-bye and bury the memory of her child. The canyon symbolized for Nancy how her life experiences had shaped who she was. Although there were scars and shadows on the sides of the canyon, a river flowed through it and the sunlight reflected the beauty of the canyon walls.

For her memorial, Patty chose to purchase toys for the children's hospital in her community. She does this every year on the anniversary of her baby's due date. Other post-abortion women memorialize their children by planting a tree, erecting a small wooden cross in the mountains; purchasing "in memory of" plaques, holding "official" memorial services with friends, family, or other post-abortion women; writing songs and poems or painting pictures. Choose the memorial that seems right and at a time that is appropriate for you.

RECONCILING WITH OTHERS

The second part of bringing closure to your abortion experience is reconciling with others. Working through personal forgiveness issues was the first part in this process, and for some that may be the only thing you need to do in order to reconcile with others. Forgiveness is in itself a reconciliation process. Whether or not you talked with someone directly, forgiving them or asking for forgiveness through God may have given you the closure you needed in that relationship.

Sometimes it is not possible to reconcile with someone directly. You may have lost all contact with the father of the baby, you may not know who the doctor was that performed your abortion, or it may be harmful for you or the other person to have contact with one another. In situations like these, you may want to write a letter you don't send, or use your journal to say what needs to be said.

In Monique's case there was some reconciliation, but no restoration of the relationship. Monique wrote a letter to

Peter about her feelings and her need for closure. She asked him to call her if he felt he could talk with her about the abortion and their relationship. Peter did call, and they were able to share with one another. Both Monique and Peter were able to ask each other for forgiveness and give that gift to one another. With all of her reconciliation behind her, Monique felt completely free to close the door on her abortion experience.

Closure symbolizes a fresh new morning. How wise of God to give us day and night. Many days people wish for more time to get things done; however, at the end of a long and hard day they are more than grateful for it to come to an end. Somehow a fresh perspective is gained with the next new day. With this change comes an untried beginning, true movement toward growth. But this change can't happen until we have closure. The sun must go down and the clock strike midnight before a new morning can begin.

We encourage you to look up and see your dawn. A new beginning, a new life . . . better, fuller, and more complete.

We share with you some poems written by clients as they brought closure to their abortion:

The Rose

Eyes of experience piercing through;
The wide-eyed innocence;
Drawing out the woman within.
The bloom unfolding, hesitant.

Sorrow for the rose, picked too soon.
Child of yellow sunshine;
Child of winter, solitude and pain.

The bud picked, shall it ever attain
To the grandeur which was once
Its promise?
Nay—its petals crumbed and brown:
It lies dead on the ground.

Awake, my Rose, and see;
The glory meant for thee!
That which the past had pledged to be;
A shadow of reality.

Jeri S. Turner
1990, Denver
Used by Permission

To My Child

How can I say I'm sorry
For the chance you never had,
To know and see and feel
All that your Father had planned?
So innocent was your existence,
So worthy in His sight.
What evilness deceived me
Into thinking it was right?
How can I tell you I love you
If that love you never knew?
What can I do to show you
That I really was thinking of you?
My accusers cry out "Murder."
How quickly they condemn;
But comfort or solace offered me
By so very few of them.
How can you ever forgive me?
I confess the injustice was grave.
If only another chance I'd have,
A road of love for you I'd pave.
Rest in His love, my child,
For it is perfect and complete
And we shall meet again, dear child,
At our Savior's feet.

Karen Sherer
Used by Permission

My sweet young daughters,
>How often I long for you!
>Taking you from the hidden place
>>in my heart I hold you up into
>>the light whispering my words
>>to you,

My oldest, my first,
>Too young and weak was I then
>>unable to nurture your tender
>>soul to growth with these hands
>>of mine

To see your smile; to know
>your fervor
>I wish to thank your people for
>their loving.

My baby, my last,
>The fear, the silence swept you
>>away like a tidal wave,
>>mingling forever your dying
>>and my shame.
>To hold you dear, rocking you
>to sleep.
>I cry to say I love you; the deepest
>loss I'll ever bear.

Daughters of mine, I hold you in my
heart's memory until we meet again.

> Penny

(Note: The oldest child was relinquished
for adoption. The baby was aborted.)

PART THREE

❧

Hope for

---

the

Journey

CHAPTER THIRTEEN

Where Do I Go from Here?

> Its hard to believe the freedom we find
> from the things we leave behind.[1]

"Where do I go from here?" may be a question you are still wondering about. Questions like these arise: "Will my abortion come back to haunt me?" "Will the pain ever be completely gone?" "Will I always feel sad when I see children?" "Will I get to the place where I'm confident of forgiveness, where I'm not trying to make up for or replace my lost child?"

Many people who move have difficulty when the time comes to pack. It's tough to go through the contents of a house you have lived in for several years. Memories, familiar people, places, and sights, even familiar daily routines will be left behind. Yet while you're packing and cleaning you rid yourself of so much accumulated "stuff." While sorting through your things you may wonder, "Why did I keep this?" or "I remember when this . . ." As this happens memories will come—some good and some bad. Many of these need to be left behind, as it were, in the old house.

How you deal with your life today is in part determined by how much of the past remains undealt with. In "Looking for Suzanne," songwriter Trisha Walker captured this with the lines:

> When there are pieces of our lives left unattended,
> and scars of broken hearts go unmended,
> then the feelings we've forgotten
> overtake us like a flood.[2]

You have acknowledged, grieved, and let go of the emotions and pain surrounding your abortion. You have grieved for your child and have said good-bye. In a way you have packed up, discarded, reorganized, and moved; you now can learn to readjust. Indeed there is freedom in laying aside and leaving behind burdens carried too long.

It's time to move into your new life. Yes, the past will always be part of your life, for it has shaped you in significant ways. Learning to integrate, but not carry, your abortion takes a while. Integrating is similar to moving. You know that the loss is a part of your history, but now your life is not being controlled by the sorrow. You may have carried your abortion alone for many years; it took up space in your mind and heart. Moving means making some changes.

Even though you have moved past your abortion, you sometimes think about your baby. A thought is triggered, a moment remembered. This always happens when you leave someone or something behind. Life is indeed a journey and can only be lived one day at a time. We strive, as we hope you will, to live in the present, look toward the future, and learn from the past.

At one time the abortion experience so consumed and overwhelmed you that you may fear it will happen again. But, what once consumed your time and your energy is no longer there. If you have faced your emotions and done the work of grieving in this book, your abortion loss does not have to overwhelm you again. You will have moments of reflection, regret, and memory, for they are part of the normal grieving process for all who experience significant loss. Reminders do not mean relapse.

Luci shares this story to illustrate what we mean:

> Several years ago, Penny and I were in Washington, D.C., on business. We took an afternoon off to visit the National Gallery at the Smithsonian. Penny wanted to see a special generations exhibit. I wanted to see African rugs and artifacts, so we went our separate ways, agreeing on a time and place to meet later.

At some point, I looked up and saw Penny across the room. We found a private corner and she told me, "I saw a picture of a little girl with dark curly hair and beautiful eyes in the exhibit. I realized that I never will have a picture of the child I aborted!"

Later we took a long walk outdoors. Penny talked about what it felt like to know that there never would be a picture, something to hold and cherish.

She let the tears of regret come then. I knew she needed me with her as she experienced the loss. As we got on the train to return to our hotel, she said, "I know this doesn't mean I'm not healed. All that grief work I did was not in vain. This is a new realization, an area of loss I had recognized but not felt in my heart." She was able to process her feelings and her memories, *but* the entire abortion experience did not come flooding back to overwhelm her.

Because Penny has entered into a relationship with God through Christ, she has great hope and anticipation that after death she will also be with God. On that day she will see her aborted child—really see her, hug, love, and talk with her. Until then, God gave her the gift of a mental picture.

Memories or new realizations will come and will bring up many different feelings. The emotions of grief will not feel as intense as they have in the past; however, there will probably be a feeling of sadness that is familiar. Two things are important to remember as you work through these memories: First, hold on to the truth and remind yourself of how far you've come. Second, acknowledge and talk or write about the incidents as they arise so that they can also be healed and integrated.

You can have a healthy life. You are capable of processing, integrating, and moving beyond your painful memories and emotions. We know this process works. What we want and believe God wants is for you to be free to embrace the rest of your life fully without reservation.

FINISHING

During the 1992 summer Olympics, a runner who had trained for years was a contender for the gold. With the finish line in sight, Eric Redmond fell face down, his hamstring torn. With no chance of winning, he struggled to his feet, and began limping toward the finish line. He knew the gold was out of the question, but Eric wanted to reach the finish line no matter what.

Suddenly, a man—his father as it turned out—jumped from the stands and ran up to Eric. As millions watched, it was as if this father said, "Son, you can stop. You don't have to keep going." Eric only shook his head. As he put his son's arm around his shoulders, Eric's dad gave his son and the world this message: "Okay, let's go. I started this with you. I'll finish it with you."

And together they finished the race. There was no gold medal, but medals fade. The love of this father will shine forever in the eyes of his son and all who watched that day.

Eric had a great advantage. His dad was there with him, encouraging and loving him. During his years of training his father was at all the races to support his son. This dad believed in his son and wanted his dream to come true. He started and finished the race with him. Do you wonder if Eric actually could have hobbled alone to the finish line? We—and many others—doubt he would have made it without his dad to help. We have come to believe in and rely on the unconditional, certain, and never-ending love that God has for us. We believe God is a lot like Eric Redmond's dad. He wants to be there for us whether we are running, hobbling, or fallen. . . .

We believe He sent His son, the man called Jesus, to earth to save and heal everyone who will let Him. Jesus was sent to show us what God, His Father, is like, for Jesus is the exact image of God. God sent Him to show us the full extent of His love and concern. Because Jesus is Savior, we can renew our relationship with God through Him—and then God becomes our Father also. No matter what your earthly father was like, you can be "adopted" into a new family with a new Father.

In our life experience, as well as perhaps in you life, there has been pain and broken relationship with your father.

Men, like women, have unmet needs, pain baggage, and too few healthy role models. Consequently, since time began they have not lived up to their responsibilities. Our parents are supposed to model for us an image or idea about who God is. When our parents, particularly our fathers, fail to nurture and protect us, it causes us to have difficulty in entering into a relationship with God as a parent. If this is where you are, we hope that you will be able to move past your current perception of man and father. Please don't let it keep you from a relationship with the perfect one. . .friend and lover. All men fail. . .God does not. *He is a different kind of man.*

We hope you will see yourself in the following stories and come to know this man Jesus who loves His people regardless of who they are or what they've done. He loves us all. You are a one of a kind treasure to God. Your life has value and purpose no matter how far off course you have wandered. He loves you enough to come all the way down from the stands to be beside you and to help you. The people in these stories had powerful, life changing relationships with Jesus. We are not asking you to look to "religion," but rather the person and character of the "God who became man" named Jesus. He loves you and wants nothing in return, except to be with you until the finish line is crossed.

A WOMAN NAMED MARY

Her name could have been Mary, Janet, or Susanne. In today's world, she may be called a prostitute because she gave sexual favors to men. Sometimes she got paid and sometimes she didn't. The only type of relationship she had with these men was physical—no commitment, no intimacy, no love, and no respect. She was used for their pleasure and sent away. They went on with their life and she went on to be used again.

The Jewish law said it was wrong to commit adultery. In fact, the law stated that if a woman was caught in the act she would be stoned. One day some self-righteous men tried to catch this young woman in the act. They wanted to see how the teacher of God's love would react, so they brought her to Jesus to test Him.

They gathered in a big circle around her and asked Jesus what He thought should be done to "such a woman." Jesus thought for a while as He looked into each face and then suggested to the men that whichever one of them had never sinned could throw the first stone at her.

One by one they all put down their rocks and went home. Only Jesus and the woman were left. He said, "Where are they? Could not one of them condemn or stone you?" She replied, "They are all gone but you. Will you stone me?" Jesus, with compassion and love in His voice, said, "No, I do not condemn you. You are free to go and leave your life of sin and sorrow."

From that moment on this woman's life was changed forever—because she had received unconditional freedom from a man who wanted nothing in return. He showed her respect, concern, love, and understanding as she had never known from any man before. His message spoke comforting words to her heart: "You were made for things better than this. You are worth more than this. I can give you back your self-respect. Leave your old lifestyle. Follow the truth, the life, and the way" (see John 8:2–11).

This woman did leave her old life, because of love, not laws. She lived the remainder of her life deeply devoted to Jesus. She spent time with Him and His friends, listened to His every word and became the person He created her to be. She loved Him because of how He had loved her. Does your heart long for someone to love you like this?

Broken Believer

> She sits alone when the day is done
> She tries to pray but the words just won't come
> 'Cause life sometimes finds a way of breaking hearts
>   and dreams
> Making it hard to believe

Broken believer
Hold on tight
Through the nights when you're so afraid
'Cause in His hands He holds
All the pieces to your heart
Let His healing start
Broken believer

There will be times when you'll feel forsaken
But the Lord is with you, though your heart
    is breaking
When you just can't see that hope will come at last
'Cause you're blinded by the failures of the past

Broken believer
Hold on tight
Through the nights when you're so afraid
'Cause in His hands He holds
All the pieces to your heart
Let His healing start
Broken believer

If you put your life into His hands
There's healing in His scars
He can touch the deepest wound
And mend your broken heart

Broken believer
Hold on tight
Through the nights when you're so afraid
'Cause in His hands He holds
All the pieces to your heart
Let His healing start
Broken believer[3]

KING DAVID

David was the youngest and the weakest child in his family. He was a shepherd boy who spent most of his days alone with his sheep, but he was the one chosen by God to be King of Israel. David's most important quality was his humble heart, not his political savvy, his military strength, or his career goals. Throughout his life, David made major mistakes, but his heart remained open to hearing God. David wanted God's plan to shape his life.

As a shepherd boy, David spent many nights alone out in the hills. During that time and throughout his life David wrote many of the psalms in the Bible. Someone has said there is a psalm for every feeling you will ever have. David felt and expressed all of his emotions: fear, joy, anger, sorrow, peace, guilt, excitement. No matter what the situation he found himself in, he shared it with his God. He wrote about his experiences and his emotions for his people to sing, and the book of Psalms is the result. David understood that God knew his deepest thoughts and loved him no matter what they were.

In some psalms you hear David saying, "Give thanks to the LORD, for He is good" (Ps. 107:1); "The LORD is good and his love endures forever" (Ps. 100:5 NIV). And in others: "In my anguish I cried to the Lord and he answered me by setting me free" (Ps. 118:5 NIV); "I am poor and needy, and my heart is wounded within me" (Ps. 109:22 NIV), and "Why have you rejected me?" (Ps. 43:2 NIV).

What David had was faith in and knowledge of the character of God. He knew if he confessed sin, admitted his doubt and fear, asked for wisdom, and was thankful, God would meet him in all of these places, love him, and give him the exact help he needed. Do you ever want to be honest and share your feelings with someone who could hear everything and still love you?

LAZARUS, MARY, AND MARTHA

Jesus liked being at the home of Lazarus and his two sisters, Mary and Martha. When he needed a place of refuge, Jesus would go to their house. It was warm and safe, and no doubt He felt loved, accepted, and comfortable there.

Then while Jesus was out of town teaching, Lazarus got sick, really sick. Mary and Martha were frightened that their brother would die. They were also sure Jesus could prevent this so they sent word to Him. "Come quickly, the one you love is dying," they beseeched Him (see John 11:1–46).

It took Jesus three days to get there. In that time Lazarus did die and was already buried by the time Jesus arrived. Three days to come for His dearest friends when they needed Him. Does that make sense? You would think He would have dropped everything to get there.

Mary and Martha were weeping bitterly and grieving for their brother when Jesus finally arrived. Jesus began to weep with the sisters and then He had a strange conversation with Mary about life and death. He asked her if she believed Lazarus would live again. Mary told Him yes that Lazarus would live again at the end of time. She also told Him that if He had come earlier, Lazarus wouldn't have died. She must have felt that if God really loved them He would not have allowed Lazarus to die.

However, this is not the end of the story. In demonstrating what the whole purpose of His life was about, Jesus raised Lazarus from the dead. He could have come in time to prevent Lazarus' death, but He wanted to let people know the true power of His love. Do you wish you knew someone who could make the dead live again?

The Healer

Bring Me all your sorrows, children, I will take your pain,
Let Me calm your throbbing heart and let you live again.
I know what you're feeling and the pain that came before,
I understand that you have been through the coals of Hell
    and more.

For I'm the Healer and I will set you free,
I gave My all to loose your soul
When I died on Calvary.

Immerse in Me your cleansing wound, the nails in your soul,
For in My resurrected hands and feet your wounds are whole.
The hurt and pain, the anguish in your heart, the heavy load,
Come, I am the oasis. Drop your burdens by the road.

For I'm the Healer and I will set you free,
I gave My all to loose your soul
When I died on Calvary.

Let Me raise you from the dust, restore you once again,
Return you to the glory that was first inborn in man.
Impossible, you may think it, to dissolve your guilt and shame,
But I am Christ the Healer, what I made I'll make again.[4]

We too have wished we had a dad who would be there for us every step of the way, to cheer us on, to pick us up, and to help us to the finish line. We have also wanted someone to love us unconditionally, and someone with whom we could honestly share our feelings.

We have wished that the things inside our hearts that were wounded and dead could come alive again. And in the search for answers to these questions we found that in our relationship with Jesus, He and His father have been able to supply the desires of our hearts.

Some books have been particularly helpful to us in understanding who Jesus is and how fulfilling our life could be in partnership with Him. We list them here as an encouragement to you:

1. The gospel of Luke in the Bible is a good place to read more about the life of Jesus and to find out who He really is.

2. *Divine Romance* by Gene Edwards is an allegory about how and why God created man. The story shows how our relationship with God was meant to be a great romance, beginning with creation and ending when Jesus comes back to finally destroy evil.

3. *Hinds' Feet in High Places* by Hannah Hurnard is another wonderfully written allegory about God's love for His children and their yearning for joy, love, and strength. The story is based on a journey to the High Places, by a young girl named Much Afraid, who gains, among other things, a New Name.

4. *Six Hours One Friday, God Came Near*, and *No Wonder They Call Him Savior* are three books written by Max Lucado about Jesus' life. All contain short chapters that can stand alone as essays about Jesus.

5. *The Chronicles of Narnia* by C. S. Lewis is an allegory about Jesus. Four children travel from their home in World War II England to a magical land where Aslan the Lion battles evil. These seven books are classics for adults and children.

6. *Ragman and Other Cries of Faith* by Walter Wangerin, Jr. contains short stories about the power of Jesus in everyday life.

Where do you go from here? We close with these words from songwriter Michael Card:

> The beginning will make all things new
> New life belongs to Him
> He hands us each new moment saying,
> My child, begin again
> My child, begin again
> You're free to start again.[5]

Our prayer is that you begin again now and step into a new life. We pray that you would come to know and rely on God's incredible love—may He be with you each moment of every day, refreshing, renewing, and restoring you . . . may He bless your going out and your coming in.

Luci and Penny

Appendix A

1. We admitted we were powerless over alcohol—that our lives had become unmanageable.

2. Came to believe that a Power greater than ourselves could restore us to sanity.

3. Made a decision to turn our will and our lives over to the care of God as we understood Him.

4. Made a searching and fearless moral inventory of ourselves.

5. Admitted to God, to ourselves, and to another human being the exact nature of our wrongs.

6. Were entirely ready to have God remove all these defects of character.

7. Humbly asked Him to remove our shortcomings.

8. Made a list of all persons we had harmed, and became willing to make amends to them all.

9. Made direct amends to such people wherever possible, except when to do so would injure them or others.

10. Continued to take personal inventory and when we were wrong promptly admitted it.

11. Sought through prayer and meditation to improve our conscious contact with God as we understood

Him, praying only for knowledge of His will for us and the power to carry that out.

12. Having had a spiritual awakening as the result of these steps, we tried to carry this message to alcoholics, and to practice these principles in all our affairs.

Appendix B

Intensive Care

In our world almost everybody "looks good." They hide their need for love and hide their loneliness—and most of them hide it very well. Reading this book may be the first time you ever realized that you were not the only one who has fought with the memories, emotions, and pain over your abortion.

Victoria was forty when she began to realize that her attempts at doing all the right things, church involvement, and volunteer work were not filling the hole in her heart. Drinking uncontrollably every Thanksgiving through Christmas bothered her, and it seemed that she had no ability or energy to relate to her husband or children. She had told only her husband about the two abortions she had years earlier, and no one about the oppressive heaviness she felt constantly.

Victoria finally broke the silence and told her trusted friend, Joan. Joan did not condemn or push Victoria but suggested she might need to get some help. Within a few months of sharing with Joan, Victoria entered therapy. As she slowly revealed her painful and abusive past, Victoria found another real confidante in her therapist. When the therapist suggested that a group might be helpful, Victoria panicked. It was difficult enough for her to share with three people who didn't know each other; she couldn't imagine telling a whole roomful of women. But eventually, Victoria decided to try a group for women with abusive pasts. Victoria soon became friends with a couple of the women in her group. She also found the group to be a safe and nurturing experience. The next year Victoria participated in a group specifically to work on Post-Abortion Stress. She completed two post-abortion groups and now coleads groups of other women.

Victoria needed acceptance and unconditional love. She did not need to be rushed, but she welcomed the gentle challenge by people who had proved they would stick with her even if she didn't get better fast. Time and long-term intensive care helped Victoria find relief and release from her past crises. Victoria had to take some pretty scary risks, make some mistakes, and go slowly. And she'd be the first to tell you it was worth it all. Today she feels unburdened and more whole than she ever thought possible.

WHOM YOU WANT AND WHOM YOU NEED

Very few people are good at gut-level intimacy. They need a great deal of respect and consistency in relationships before they open up to share their deep concerns, and that is as it should be. We hope you will be able to look among your friends, family, or community to find someone to risk being honest with. It is important that whoever you confide in be a person of integrity and reliability. We also rank the quality of "being real" very high on our list of positive character traits.

Often the person you really want to be there for you in your grief may not be capable of that right now. Many times our clients decide that the father of the baby or a special man in their lives is supposed to know what they need and be there to provide love and support and share the loss with an intensity that matches theirs. Maybe he "should," but often he cannot or will not. Many fathers have come to feel the pain and share the loss, yet many others refuse to allow it to touch them. They respond in this way for the same reasons you have sheltered yourself, although men and women generally respond to emotional pain differently. One day we suspect the grief will impact him, but you cannot force it.

Just as you came to see your neediness and sought help, we hope he will also.

Consider the reason you seem so set on one particular person helping you. In your diligence to get your needs met in one way, are you rejecting other folks who are willing and capable of providing what you really need?

Not everyone understands grief. This lack of understanding and not knowing what to do or say often causes people to avoid anyone who is suffering or dealing with loss. We're not sure anyone can truly understand until they have experienced loss and grief at some level. If you have been in the intensive care waiting room of a hospital or at a funeral home with someone you loved, then you do understand.

Who might be able to comfort you? Some possibilities are a trusted friend, parent, family member, counselor, pastor, another post-abortion woman, the father of the baby, or your current partner. It is important to find the right person for you right now.

QUALITIES FOR YOUR SUPPORT PERSON

We have talked about the qualities we feel are important for healthy relationships: trust, respect, honesty, and loyalty. We also suggest you consider certain qualities if you are looking for a counselor or a support group to help you work through your grief:

1. Confidentiality. You need the assurance that what you share will be held in strict confidence.

2. Respect for your personal convictions and feelings.

3. Knowledge and respect for the process of grieving. That means no quick-fix solutions.

4. A degree of professionalism that balances itself with a willingness to enter into a relationship with you.

5. Clear and healthy boundaries that are not violated.

6. An ability to share in your pain but not become overwhelmed by it.

7. A belief in your ability to know what your issues are and the pace you need to take in resolving them.

Following are some questions that you might use in searching for and interviewing a counselor. Good therapists will not mind being asked these questions or any others you may want to add.

Questions for a Therapist

1. Can you have a free introduction interview to ask questions?

2. What is their knowledge about and experience with these topics:
   Post-Abortion Stress issues
   Post Traumatic Stress Disorder
   Women
   Grief work
   Abuse
   Addictions
   Spiritual issues

3. What are their feelings and beliefs about these issues?
   Abortion
   Post-Abortion Stress

4. What theories and techniques do they use in counseling?

5. How do they handle confidentiality issues?

6. How do they define a professional relationship?

7. Ask for references and check them out.

THE INTENSIVE CARE RELATIONSHIP

Our clients have found the support they needed in many different ways with different people in their lives.

It was difficult for Sharon to go to a post-abortion group because her husband, who was not the father of the baby, did not understand why she needed to work this out. He thought that because Sharon's abortion had happened several years ago, she should put it behind her and he believed that when things are over you don't look back. He loved Sharon as she was and felt cheated because he was having to deal with the pain someone else had caused her.

Sharon persisted in attending group but never put undue expectations on her husband. She knew his love was strong and that he would support her even though he couldn't understand. The group and her journal writing were very helpful for her. She let her husband know that he could read the journal if and when he wanted to. He wanted to understand so he did read it from time to time. He became more compassionate as he saw in writing his wife's pain.

Both Sharon and her husband needed someone to care about their personal feelings. Try to understand when someone you love is not as ready as you are to deal with your loss. Remember, it took you a while to get where you are today.

Another client, Joanne, and her husband, Jim, dealt with her abortion together. Joanne had an abortion in a previous marriage many years before she met Jim. Their counselor shared one of her sessions with them in this note:

Jim had come several times with Joanne to her counseling sessions. Today Joanne wanted to reconcile with the baby and say good-bye. I knew it would be intense, so I was a little shocked to see Jim with her. What a wonderful experience it was for me to see him be completely supportive throughout the session.

She cried from the moment we began. At several points, I would see Jim reach for the tissue box. He was sharing her pain, hurting with and alongside her. As Joanne moved through the process of naming and saying good-bye to her baby, Jim was part of the experience. Now it was integrated into both their lives and the experience was held sacred by each of them.

Gloria and Dan had been sweethearts since seventh grade. In their junior year of high school she got pregnant and together they chose abortion as a solution to their problem. They kept this secret from everyone and married soon after graduation. When Gloria and Dan had their first child, they realized what they had lost and that they needed to grieve for the child they had aborted. They found a group for post-abortion couples in the local newspaper listings for support groups. Today, as a couple they share their past and the process of healing with others.

These stories illustrate different places and ways you can find help. You deserve to grieve, and having someone to care for you during this time is vital.

In many cities around the country, hospitals have set up phone lines intended to assist citizens of the community in finding doctors and other health care. We wish we could provide you with a "Care-Finder" network similar to the one in Nashville. You need a special person or group of people who will care for you intensely through the grieving and healing process. We encourage you to persist in your search until you find the right people. Not everyone understands pain, grief, and loss, and even fewer understand them as they relate to Post-Abortion Stress. At the same time, there are people all over the United States and the world who do understand and want to help.

Your burden can be lifted, this sorrow and pain will not last forever. Take someone's hand and dare to walk into your grief. If you follow the path to the end, you will find the treasures of a renewed life waiting.

A MESSAGE FOR THE CARE GIVER

Streams of Mercy

Go in peace, I said to my friend
I'm not the one you were seeking after all
Here's your release from my anger and my
    failure
I thought you knew, it's only hot air, after all.

Strong arms are waiting
The lover of my soul
Who will let me live
Where streams of mercy flow.

Without a word, or with one too many
Either way, I got the message loud and clear
I do defer and I'll say it was easy
While my witness starts to crumble, loud and
    clear.

Strong arms are waiting
The lover of my soul
Who will let me live
Where streams of mercy flow.

In calm waters, I am shrinking
Down to size
Tender hands lift me up
And hold me like a prize.

Strong arms are waiting
The lover of my soul
Who will let me live
Where streams of mercy flow.[1]

What does a woman who suffers Post-Abortion Stress need from a friend like you? We think the song "Streams of Mercy" clearly defines what this woman needs: strong arms, someone to love her soul, hands to lift her up, and to live in mercy. We can share some thoughts from our experience to guide you in caring for your friend in this painful place.

There is hope and healing from her pain. She can get through this grief and embrace life again with new energy and joy. We believe working through the process outlined in this book, plus having a support person like yourself, is the key.

Your friend is experiencing grief. It is important that she be allowed to grieve the loss of her aborted child and any other loss she feels. In fact, it is essential if she is to move beyond her past. Your most important gift to her is validating her loss.

In *A Grief Observed* C. S. Lewis chronicles his grief over the loss of his wife and makes a profound observation, "The one thing you cannot do alone is grieve."

Judith Viorst in her remarkable book *Necessary Losses*, quotes a grieving person who says, "I need to know that there is someone besides myself who really cares if I live or die." And "What I need is a sacred and miraculous connection called friendship."[2]

So what we want you to know is that you are important; in fact in our view, you are essential. In some respects it is an honor to be allowed into the heart of grief. Please know that your presence, your *being with her*, is the best gift you can offer.

The big issues for those in grief are loneliness and a fear that their pain will overwhelm them. Actively grieving is the way to relieve the ache.

Probably the most common mistake helpers make is trying to fix the situation or the feeling. You don't want your friends to suffer. You look for formulas, six easy steps, the right words, gifts, distractions, and other ways to help stop the grief. However, the only way out is through the grief process.

You need to skip your agenda and time frame. Your friend needs time—time to feel her loss. One thing is sure: grief cannot be rushed. It's possible that the longer grief stays inside, the longer it takes to heal. Your part is providing a confidential, safe, caring place for this to happen.

It's important that you give her the freedom to move at her own pace, not pressuring too hard to move on. That's a fine line since being a real friend sometimes means you need to encourage movement with some gentle confrontation. As in all good relationships, it's important to know that everything is done in love, acceptance, respect, and confidentiality.

There may be times when you will have to work at balancing your own emotion and logic. It is easy to become uncomfortable or overwhelmed by heavy doses of emotion.

Anger, depression, and sorrow are very intense feelings. We encourage you to take care of yourself.

It's important to set clear boundaries concerning your abilities and availabilities. Remember that you are not her savior—you will not have all the answers—you cannot stop her pain or fix her. That is the work of God and the grieving process.

Above all, what you can do is hold onto the hope and belief that healing and movement will take place as the path through the valley of grief is taken. The blessing you receive from giving and sharing will be greater than the time and love you've spent.

Appendix C

Your Support Group

Being able to work through emotional and grief issues in a support group environment is very effective for many people. Although a group experience may seem a little scary for some women, often the benefits outweigh the initial discomfort. Groups tend to help women for several reasons.

BENEFITS OF A GROUP

The first benefit of a group is that it breaks isolation, that "I'm-all-alone" feeling. Group brings you into a community of people who share your experience. This provides one of the most effective ways to receive validation for your feelings and support during your grieving and healing process.

The second benefit of a group experience is the accountability factor. When there are other people to help keep you on track and challenge you, you are more likely to make it through the hard spots. The other group members can offer you hope and become your safety net. Because of your common abortion experiences, trust and bonding are easier.

The last major advantage of a group is the greater speed with which your healing can take place. The healing process tends to move faster in a group setting because of the shared expression of feelings. When one group member shares, it is common for other members' emotions to be tapped. You are then able to deal with the same issue either during the group process or at a later time.

TYPES OF GROUPS

There are essentially two types of groups. The first type of group is a group therapy situation that has a professional group leader. The second type is a support group where there is no designated leader; all members of the support group colead. Those women dealing with post-abortion grief issues can benefit from either type of group.

You could choose either type of group, depending on your particular needs and desires. The material in this appendix can be adapted to fit a support or therapy group. Note that a therapy group will be better suited to deal with other issues that may come up during the healing process. We also strongly recommend that each person in a support group make a commitment to seek professional help if they become overwhelmed in group, feel suicidal, or begin abusing drugs or alcohol. Group members need to hold each other accountable.

We recommend that if you are considering a group with a professional leader that there be two group facilitators. Teamwork benefits the group because the diverse qualities of two different leaders enable them to attend to any situation that may arise, as well as give individual attention to a group member without unduly taking away from the other members. Characteristics to look for in group leaders are compassion, a working knowledge of group dynamics, grief issues, post-abortion issues, and a personal experience with abortion or some other loss issue that they have worked through.

GROUP STRUCTURE

In setting up and organizing a group, a few suggestions will be helpful.

The number of women in the group should ideally be between five and eight; this number is ideal for the group process. Too few participants cause a breakdown in group dynamics if women drop out or are unable to attend every meeting. Too many women in the group make it hard for everyone to share their ideas and feelings.

After the first session, the group should become closed to new members. This is necessary to help build trust, continuity, and ensure confidentiality. Women should make a commitment to the group by the second meeting and be willing to attend all group meetings.

We recommend a commitment from eight to twelve weeks with one meeting per week. We find that one and a half to two hours time per meeting is optimum. The length of time the group meets depends on a variety of factors: the number of participants, the rate at which the members are willing to work, the number of issues which arise. Ask the group to pencil in an additional session or two on their calendars in case it becomes necessary to extend the group experience. Try not to have an extra session unless *all* group members can attend. It should not be necessary to go past twelve weeks.

Groups work best if the members have similar ties (age, background, marital status). However, as long as there is someone else in the group to identify with either in background or personality, some diversity doesn't seem to create problems for the women in the group.

Hold the meetings at a central location for the group members. It is very important for the meeting place to be private and comfortable. Pay attention to furnishings, privacy, safety for night meetings, lighting, etc. A comfortable, homey atmosphere helps when dealing with hard issues.

Reading and discussing one chapter of the book at a time will work for a group that wants to meet twelve times. If you want to meet for a shorter period we recommend you break the book up as follows: Chapter 1 and 2 at first meeting; Chapter 3 and 4 for the second meeting; then one chapter a week thereafter. Note that this does not include an introductory meeting to discuss format, meeting place, rules, etc. Remember to read chapters before each meeting.

GROUP RULES

All group members should be aware of and abide by the common group rules. This can be talked about at the beginning of the first meeting.

1. Confidentiality is a must. Nothing said in group should be talked about outside group. You may also decide to keep the identity of group members confidential.

2. To gain maximum benefit from the process and in respect to the other group members, it would be best if all group participants agreed to come each time the group meets. An agreement should also be made to read the chapters and do the work required. Encourage each other when it seems difficult to come to the meetings.

3. If a group member finds it necessary to leave the group, she should be willing to let the group know the reason for dropping out. Everyone should feel free to leave if the need arises.

4. Practicing good communication skills helps each group member share her ideas and feelings as well as feel supported and validated by the group.

   a. Give positive non-judgmental feedback, using "I" statements. Remember that feelings are neither good nor bad.

   b. Don't rescue one another. Sit with each other in your painful times. Affirm feelings and avoid the temptation to give each other a quick fix.

   c. Be active listeners. Don't interrupt one another. After someone has shared, each group member who would like to respond can then talk, describing what was happening for them as the other person shared her story and insights.

d. Give everyone in the group a chance to participate. Some people find it easy to talk; others are more shy. There should not be a heavy expectation for people to share. Even women who have little to say during group benefit greatly. However, "talkers" must be sensitive to how much of the group's time they are taking up, while those who would normally hang back and just listen must make the effort to participate verbally.

GROUP FORMAT

The basic format for each group meeting is to discuss the information from each chapter. The group members read the specific chapter and work through any homework from that chapter before group. During group you share with each other your thoughts, feelings, and questions concerning the material in that chapter. If at any point the group feels that one meeting was not enough time to cover the topics covered in the chapter, you can opt to continue for one more meeting. This is most likely to happen with the anger and reconciliation chapters.

Not everyone will process information at the same rate. Try not to get stuck on one issue, however. One of the goals of group work is to move through the entire healing process so that when things come up later you will be aware of how the process works. Hopefully it will become a positive way to deal with issues throughout your life.

During the first meeting you should:

1. Talk about the group rules.

2. Spend some time getting to know one another.

3. Talk about the purpose of the group. The group is a safe place for each person to share the pain of her past abortion experience, to deal with the feelings and grief issues associated with her abortion, to experience forgiveness, and lastly, to learn how to

successfully cope with the ongoing reminders of her abortion experience.

4. Set some group and individual goals. You can brainstorm about what you each would like to get out of group, areas where you really need to focus, behaviors you might want to change, and what healing would look like for you. Looking back at these goals at the end of group helps you recognize your growth as well as identify any areas you can continue to work on.

In the subsequent meetings we suggest starting each meeting with a "round." For one or two minutes each member takes a turn and talks about how she is, her feelings about the abortion, the homework, or what kind of week it has been. You pick only one topic or question each meeting for the "round." This helps to bond and focus the group.

It is important to recognize and affirm each group member. We make an effort to recognize each attempt the individual group members make to contribute to the group experience by acknowledging their comments or responding to what they have said. We also try to affirm the group members for their courage in being present in the group, the hard work they accomplish, and the growth they achieve.

At the final meeting you can go over your goal list and talk about where each person is now, what tasks she has completed, where she still needs to work, and what the group was like. You will want to talk about how each person is going to deal with the ongoing reminders and pain. We also suggest that you spend some time sharing about what each group member has uniquely given to the group or to its individual members.

Sharing your feelings and grieving in a group setting can be a very valuable experience for you. The power of coming together in relationship to minister and hold out hope for each other is the healing balm that brings meaning and purpose back to your broken life.

Appendix D

References for Counseling

Luci Freed, M.A.

Crisis Pregnancy Support Center
1915 1/2 Church Street
Nashville, TN 37203

Penny Y. Salazar-Phillips, L.C.S.W.

Alternatives Pregnancy Center
1860 Larimer Street, #200
Denver, CO 80210

Minirth and Meier Clinics

1-800-545-1819

Focus on the Family

(719) 531-3400

Note: Staff members at Focus on the Family give no long-term counseling, but they do give referrals.

Appendix E

References for Further Reading

Anger:

Carter, Dr. Les and Dr. Frank Minirth. *The Anger Workbook*. Nashville: Thomas Nelson, 1993.

Goldhor, Harriet and Phil Lerner. *The Dance of Anger*. New York: Harper & Row, 1985.

Forgiveness:

Smedes, Lewis B. *Forgive and Forget, Healing the Hurts We Don't Deserve*. New York: Pocket Books, 1986.

Grief:

Lewis, C. S. *A Grief Observed*. Englewood: Bantam, 1961.

Means, James E. *A Tearful Celebration*. Portland: Multnomah, 1990.

Viorst, Judith, *Necessary Losses*. Gold Medal: Fawcett, 1987.

Post-Abortion:

Peretti, Frank E. *Tilly*. Wheaton: Crossway Books, 1988.

Rue, Susan Sanford. *Will I Cry Tomorrow*. Old Tappan: Revel, 1986.

Relationships:

Beattie, Melody. *Co-Dependent No More*. San Francisco: Harper-Hazelden, 1987.

Hemfelt, Dr. Robert, Dr. Frank Minirth, and Dr. Paul Meier. *Love is a Choice*. Nashville: Thomas Nelson, 1989.

Sexual Abuse:

Allender, Dan B. *The Wounded Heart*. Colorado Springs: Nav Press, 1990.

Boss, Ellen and Laura Davis. *The Courage to Heal*. New York: Harper & Row, 1988.

Frank, Jan. *Door of Hope*. Nashville: Thomas Nelson, 1987.

Shame:

Bradshaw, John. *Healing the Shame That Binds You*. Deerfield Beach: Health Communications, 1988.

Smedes, Lewis B. *Shame and Grace, Healing the Shame We Don't Deserve*. San Francisco: Zondervan, 1993.

Spiritual:

Card, Michael. *Immanuel, Reflections on the Life of Christ*. Nashville: Thomas Nelson, 1990.

Edwards, Gene. *The Divine Romance*. Auburn: Christian Books, 1985.

Hurnard, Hannah. *Hinds' Feet in High Places*. Wheaton: Tyndale, 1975.

Lewis, C. S. *The Chronicles of Narnia*. Series of 7, New York: Collier Books, 1950.

Lucado, Max. *God Came Near, Chronicles of the Christ*. Portland: Multnomah, 1987.

Lucado, Max. *In the Eye of the Storm*. Dallas: Word, 1990.

Lucado, Max. *No Wonder They Call Him the Savior*. Portland: Multnomah, 1987.

Lucado, Max. *Six Hours One Friday*. Portland: Multnomah, 1989.

Lucado, Max. *The Applause of Heaven*, Dallas: Word, 1990.

Wangerin, Walter, Jr. *Ragman and Other Cries of Faith*, San Francisco: Harper & Row, 1984.

Bible:

Book of Psalms
Book of Luke

General:

Manning, Brennan. *The Ragamuffin Gospel*. Portland: Multnomah, 1990.

Powell, John. *Fully Human Fully Alive*. Niles: Argus Communications, 1976.

Serenity: A Companion for Twelve Steps Recovery. Nashville: Thomas Nelson, 1990.

Thurman, Dr. Chris. *The Lies We Believe*. Nashville: Thomas Nelson, 1989.

Williams, Margery. *The Velveteen Rabbit*. New York: Doubleday, 1975.

Notes

Chapter 4: The Healing Process

1. James E. Means, *A Tearful Celebration* (Portland: Multnomah, 1985).

Chapter 5: Step Out of the Dark

1. C. S. Lewis, *A Grief Observed* (Englewood: Bantam, 1961).

Chapter 10: Do Not Surrender to Depression

1. Dan Allender, *The Wounded Heart* (Colorado Springs: Nav Press, 1990).

2. Lewis, *A Grief Observed.*

Chapter 11: Find Freedom in Forgiveness

1. Michael Card, "The Way of Wisdom," BMG Music Publishing Co. Used by permission.

2. *Serenity, A Companion for Twelve Step Recovery* (Nashville: Thomas Nelson, 1990).

3. Lewis B. Smedes, *Forgive and Forget: Healing the Hurts We Don't Deserve* (New York: Pocket Books, 1986).

Chapter 13: Where Do I Go from Here?

1. Michael Card, "The Things We Leave Behind," BMG Music Publishing Co. Used by permission.

2. Trisha Walker, "Looking for Suzanne," Jack & Jill Music Co., and Rebel Heart Music (ASCAP), The Welk Music Group, 1988. Used by permission.

3. Angela Pontier and Joel Lindsey, "Broken Believer," Golden Angel Music and Sidekick Music Group, 1952.

4. Jim Weber, "The Healer," Meadow Green Music Publishers, 1982. Used by permission. (Tapes are available through Touchtone Resource Group.)

5. Michael Card, "The Beginning," Bird Wing Music (ASCAP), 1989. Used by permission.

Appendix B: Intensive Care

1. Ashley Greenberg, "Streams of Mercy," Warner/ Chappell Music. Used by permission.

2. Judith Viorst, *Necessary Losses* (Gold Medal: Fawcett, 1987).

About the Authors

Penny Salazar-Phillips has been the executive director of Alternatives Pregnancy Center in Denver, Colorado, since its founding in 1982. She has a master's degree in social work and is a licensed clinical social worker in the state of Colorado. Penny uses her training and personal experience to help women who reach out to the Alternatives Pregnancy Center due to a crisis pregnancy or post-abortion stress. Her post-abortion program includes individual counseling, group therapy, and weekend retreats. Penny also trains women to develop their own post-abortion counseling programs both locally and nationally.

A Colorado native, Penny lives in Denver with her husband Kevin, son Chris, and stepson Jacob. She enjoys writing poetry, gourmet cooking, and appreciates art.

Luci Freed has a master's degree in clinical psychology, and is certified by the state of Tennessee. She has counseled families, adolescents, and women for fifteen years. Luci has been executive director of the Crisis Pregnancy Support Center in Nashville, Tennessee, for ten years. She also has a heart for teaching counseling skills and equipping post-abortion leaders. Grief work is a specialty area for her.

When not working, Luci enjoys anything outside in the sun. Her favorite activities include biking, aerobics, racquetball, and swimming. If she could fit another career into her life, she would be a landscape and flower designer.

ISBN 1-888952-10-5

6   10529 00010   0